PENGUIN BOOKS
UNBURDEN

Nithya Shanti is an internationally acclaimed teacher of joyful and conscious living. He completed an MBA from XLRI Jamshedpur and worked in the corporate world. He then went on to live as a forest meditation monk for six years. His light hearted, informal manner and practical guidance paves the way for shifts in perspective that many have found to be life-changing.

Nandini Sen Mehra is a poet and writer with an abiding curiosity about the nature of the self and the world she inhabits. A graduate in English Literature from Loreto College, Kolkata, she is also a communications professional. Nandini is the recipient of the Reuel International Poetry Prize, 2020, for Best Upcoming Poet and the author of *Whorls Within*, her debut book of poetry.

UNBURDEN

A Book *of*
Joyous Awakenings

NITHYA SHANTI
with NANDINI SEN MEHRA

PENGUIN BOOKS
An imprint of Penguin Random House

PENGUIN BOOKS

USA | Canada | UK | Ireland | Australia
New Zealand | India | South Africa | China

Penguin Books is part of the Penguin Random House group of companies
whose addresses can be found at global.penguinrandomhouse.com

Published by Penguin Random House India Pvt. Ltd
4th Floor, Capital Tower 1, MG Road,
Gurugram 122 002, Haryana, India

First published in Penguin Books by Penguin Random House India 2022

Copyright © Nithya Shanti with Nandini Sen Mehra 2022

ISBN 9780143454434

Typeset in Bembo Std and Minion Pro by Manipal Technologies Limited, Manipal
Printed at

www.penguin.co.in

For my mom, Shashi, dad, Malcolm,
all my teachers and you, dear reader.
Nithya

For Ma, Anjana Sen, and Baba, Nirendra Nath Sen.
Nandini

Contents

Section 3: A Deeper Playfulness

Introduction

In conversation with Nithya Shanti

My journey with Nithya Shanti began seven years ago, when on a whim, I attended an evening of meditation held at a home in Singapore. I had read some of his teachings, but this was my first meeting. Gentle and approachable, he carried his wisdom lightly, and I felt an instant ease in his presence. After the session concluded, we briefly spoke, and I left soon after. My warm impressions from that first interaction stayed with me, and I began to access his teachings more frequently.

Nithya visited Singapore a few more times to meet with his growing community, and I attended and organized walks through some of my favourite forest trails and had the opportunity to get to know him better. In Nithya, for the first time, I found someone who could take the most profound practices and thoughts, and lead me gently into my own exploration and discovery. In his manner of teaching, I found powerful truths simply explained, and shared with love, kindness and humour. In him, I found a teacher for our times.

I would often think how wonderful it would be to have a book of his teachings to keep with me always, as a companion, a guide, and a friend. Serendipitously, I was introduced to Premanka Goswami, the Executive Editor at Penguin Random House India and I reached out to him with the seed of an idea for a book of Nithya's teachings. To my delight, Premanka wanted to know more, and over the next year, the idea of the book took shape. Nithya, of course, simply said, 'How Wonderful!'

Assisted by able volunteers and a wonderful team of editors, the work on the book began in earnest and truly turned into a labour of love for everyone involved. For me, working on this book meant getting reacquainted with many of the central principles and ideas I had grown to love, with an opportunity to delve deeper and strengthen my own understanding and practice. It is special to have my poems open the door to each chapter, inviting the reader into a deeper exploration. I am so very grateful for the opportunity to work on this book with Nithya Shanti. I hope this book reaches many hands and hearts and becomes a gateway for readers to explore and inhabit their own lives in deeper and more joyous ways.—*Nandini*

To begin, a freewheeling conversation with Nithya Shanti.

Nandini: You decided to give up a promising corporate career for a life as a monk, returned to share what you learned, and have become a beloved teacher to thousands across the world. Did you choose the path or did the path choose you?

Nithya: It seems as I followed the breadcrumb trail of curiosity, wonder and enthusiasm, one thing unfolded after the other. At the age of sixteen, my mother was going to attend a meditation course and I decided to join her as well. I did not know it would be such a defining experience in my life. I began a regular meditation practice and noticed a remarkable shift in attention span, ability to concentrate, memory and confidence. This led to attending and serving on more meditation courses. I managed to keep my meditation practice going even during my rather demanding MBA course. As I took up a corporate job it seemed to me that my education was not yet complete. What I had learned was about getting a livelihood, not about having a meaningful life. This is why I was drawn to living as a Buddhist monk. To live a simpler life based on mindfulness and contemplation.

I am so grateful for the opportunity I have had to learn from wonderful teachers, past and present. Gradually, it became clear to me that my learnings and practice were not just for me, but for the benefit of all. I wanted to share my insights in a more open, accessible and fun way than the traditional role of a monk allowed. So, in 2008 after six years as a monk, I left my monastic life and began sharing some of my learnings with those who approached me. I would say this path called me and I chose to answer the call.

Nandini: Was there a particular moment in time when you decided you were going to be a teacher? Is the path still evolving, revealing itself to you?

Nithya: It sort of happened. I don't hold the role of a teacher very tightly. I see myself primarily as a *Kalayanamitra* or a spiritual friend. Yes, there are certain contexts in which I teach, or facilitate, or mentor, or counsel. I endeavour to not make that a big part of how I see myself. I like to see myself as a learner. As a perpetual beginner. A '*shuru*', not a 'guru'. For the beginner's mind is fresh and sees infinite possibilities, the expert's mind tends to be conditioned and only sees a few.

Nandini: Nithya, for many years you have taught all over the world, held thousands of sessions and workshops on spiritual practices and teachings, and connected with people from all walks of life, ages and religious beliefs. I'll ask you a simple question for which you may not have a simple answer. What are people looking for?

Nithya: If we ask people what they want, and then ask them why they want it, and repeat this process seven times or so, we usually get answers like: Because I want to be happy / at peace / fulfilled / free. So, in my understanding while the diversity of what we all individually want is bewildering, at the core we all want rather simple things. This recognition is important because it enables us to have empathy and compassion. Compassion means we have a common passion—we can see ourselves in others. This allows us to connect more meaningfully since shared passions are the basis of friendship, trust and goodwill. One of the reasons I feel at ease addressing any audience is that I sense that deep down they want similar things as I. So, it is as if I am speaking to a version of myself. There is ease, there is flow and there is great love.

Nandini: One of the things that I find fascinating in your teachings is the way you integrate wisdom and practices from across generations and geographies. For instance, we could be learning about a thousand-year-old Buddhist practice, and you are able to seamlessly connect it to contemporary American philosopher and writer Ken Wilber's integral theory. In your journey, who are the people you consider your most inspiring teachers?

Nithya: I consider the Buddha, Nisargadatta Maharaj and Byron Katie as my main teachers. Apart from them there are a few hundred people who have had an important role in shaping my way of looking at life for which I am deeply grateful. I consider all of them my teachers. Some I have met. Most I have not. I consider all of life as my Guru. I am a lover of wisdom more than knowledge. Wisdom implies direct experience, a willingness to hold assumptions and concepts lightly and see things from many different points of view. Perhaps curiosity, wonder and willingness to learn from others has guided me to be this way.

Nandini: What does 'Unburden' represent to you and who do you think this book is meant for?

Nithya: The title in a way captures the essential message of the book. This process is one of shedding more than accumulating. Shedding what no longer serves us. In other words, don't believe everything you think or feel. Be willing to stand back, slow down, inquire, examine different perspectives, test your assumptions in the crucible of real life. The truth is what works! Life is dynamic. Everything is constantly changing. It demands that we change as well. Suffering comes from holding on tight. When we question our thinking, when we move from personality to presence, when we access the gap between stimulus and response then we get access to a dimension of freedom and power. This is something that we can learn. It is actually learning how to unlearn! That is what this book is about.

Nandini: I find a lot of people of my generation are caught between the religious practices and rituals handed down to us by our families and our communities, and a sense of disconnection and scepticism, even cynicism about what any of it actually means. There is an awareness that perhaps there is a deeper, more authentic way to live, but the actual path seems confusing. Is there a way to integrate a spiritual life into a contemporary way of living, which demands so much of most of us?

Nithya: For a wholesome life we need to learn from our own lived experience. Religion minus fear and superstition is spirituality. It is the core or essence of religion. Each of us needs to discover our own spirituality. What resonates with us, what moves us in a deep way and can guide and orient our life. In my understanding, integrating gratitude and reflection into our everyday life is at the heart of spiritual practice. We may all have very different approaches, philosophies and beliefs when it comes to the specifics of how we do this. This diversity is actually wonderful. It makes life rich and meaningful. Keeping an open heart and mind, learning from past and present, approaching all that we learn as an opportunity to experiment and grow are some of the ways we can reimagine our spirituality.

Nandini: Most people need to earn a living. There are responsibilities, school fees, ageing parents, our own goals and aspirations. The world seems to extract a price for material success, depending on what we do; it could be time, peace of mind or even our ethics and values. Sometimes it seems as if all of this precludes any time to devote to our own selves and our spiritual journey. Must a spiritual path necessarily involve some renunciation, even if only of material ambition?

Nithya: I don't believe time used for spiritual practice is spent, I believe it is invested. The results come back compounded. We sleep better and may even need a little less sleep than we used to. We are more creative. We don't dwell on what bothers us for as long and focus on gratitude instead. Intuition guides our decision-making and we trust ourselves more. Sense of community and belonging can also get strengthened as we learn to communicate with authenticity and contribute with love. This is our primary responsibility: nourishing and nurturing all aspects of ourselves. Lack of time is usually not the issue. It is usually a matter of not prioritizing ourselves. Even a slight improvement here positively impacts the whole of our life. We need not split our life between spiritual and material pursuits. All of life can be the arena for our practice. This book explores how.

Nandini: Does one live for oneself or others? I ask this because I sense a restlessness in many. Early life choices have meant a sort of crowding in people's lives and for someone, say in their middle years, they may have awoken to a desire to live differently, to jump off the hamster wheel, but it's a path not for the faint hearted and comes with many complexities. Our decisions impact the lives of many around us, especially our loved ones. How does one reconcile to their circumstances if one cannot completely change them?

Nithya: We need not make radical life-altering choices in order to benefit from these teachings. Nor is there a need for a false dichotomy between self and other. I like the analogy of the bow and arrow. We pull back the bow string so that the arrow can fly forward straight and true. In much the same way, as we invest in ourselves our ability to support and serve others dramatically expands. There are five spaces in our life: work space, family space, leisure space, holiday space and my space.

Usually, the last one gets compromised as the demands from the other spaces seem louder or more urgent. As we begin to safeguard and prioritize our own space for self-reflection and nourishment at every level, we will find that restlessness decreases and we are in a position to be effective and of benefit wherever we are. This is how change occurs from the inside out. It leads to a more reliable transformation than abrupt changes in life circumstances, though in some cases those are also necessary. Trust where you are. There are no mistakes. With the right intentions the path becomes clear and the gumption to walk it also appears.

Nandini: I observe another predicament I see in many people, especially the young. On one hand, there is a fierce desire for independence; they do not want to be tied down, they do not want to conform to anyone else's ideas about how they must live their lives, and equally I find so many are just so lonely, with a sense of isolation, an aloneness that no amount of social media or other distractions seems to allay. What do you think is going on? Is there perhaps a need for community where people can feel they belong, without a loss of identity? A place of acceptance, a place where they feel truly seen and connected?

Nithya: Definitely a sense of community and belonging are an important part of human thriving. If we cannot find such community in the vertical dimension of our family and blood relations, then we need to seek them in the horizontal dimension of friends and those with similar values, interests and visions. While the internet and social media can contribute to loneliness, they can also enable us to discover people and communities we resonate with. When I travel around the world, I use websites and forums to find groups based on my hobbies like Frisbee and board games. We need not wait. With a little initiative, we can find meaningful connections wherever we are in the world.

Nandini: I want to talk to you a little about hope, 'that thing with feathers' as Emily Dickinson so beautifully calls it. It's apparent there is a lot going on in the world right now that could fill someone with despair. There is, of course, environmental degradation, the vast resource disparity between the wealthy and the dispossessed, issues of corruption, access, violence against women and children, the politics of money and greed, and so on and so forth. Obviously, it's a long list! Where then can one find hope and what does one do with it? It's possible some may arrive at a spiritual quest with the intention of rediscovering hope, or a purpose that will help make better sense of the world and its contradictions. I'd love your thoughts on this.

Nithya: One reason we feel disempowered is because our circle of concern is enormous and our circle of influence limited. I like to focus primarily on what is within my reach, where I can make a tangible difference. I refer to this as our local universe. Instead of worrying about wars in faraway lands which we can perhaps not do too much about, let us focus on diffusing the tensions in our own hearts and in our own families. Any progress we make here, even modest, means we are actually a part of the solution, not part of the problem. The answer comes from finding ways to expand our circle of influence and not be preoccupied with things that global media decides should be concerning us.

Nandini: As a poet, I find poetry lets me access life in a very direct way. It enables me to find the essence beneath the surface, reveal truths about the human condition that often remain concealed behind the many identities we assume. I find the entire process of poetry writing akin to meditation. So, I imagine, this might be true of anything that we do with complete devotion and surrender. What are your thoughts on different paths that may lead us in essence, to calling our own bluff?

Nithya: Yes, this is true. Anything done with presence, with love, with joy, without being too fixated on specific outcomes has a meditative quality. Meditation is less about the posture or the activity, it is primarily about being open and attentive. There are two aspects to this. One is stabilizing attention on the chosen task at hand. Second is inquiring who the doer of the task is. And who the enjoyer is. In this way, with concentration and reflection, any activity can become a meditation. It could be listening, gardening, doing the laundry, cooking a meal, taking a walk or writing poetry.

Nandini: Let's talk a little bit about identities. Some identities we inherit and some we assume. A lot of what we do, our interests, our roles, our professions define who we think we are. Do you consider our identities an impediment to spiritual growth?

Nithya: Identities are an integral part of life. We cannot deny them. However, we can learn to hold them lightly. Which means we need not be boxed in by them, defined by them, constrained by them. Like an actor who is capable of playing many kinds of roles very skilfully, we too can learn to fulfil our roles and responsibilities without getting consumed by them. Wisdom recognizes that we are more than our identities, and compassion fulfils each role with attentiveness and care. In this way, everything in our life becomes a support in our spiritual growth.

Nandini: Unburden distils a lot of your teachings from over the years. Working through the chapters with you, I found so much that seems accessible and intuitive. For me, the reason to bring this book into the world is for people to have a friend for life, a roadmap, to guide them gently and lovingly into peeling off the layers and meeting their true selves. What do you hope this book will offer our readers?

Nithya: I hope our readers gain some new perspectives and find some practices here that lighten and brighten their hearts. I wish for our readers to discover what it is like to be happy for no reason. Most of all, I hope they deeply trust their own process and see life as an incredible adventure of consciousness and not merely as a never-ending list of to-dos, and duties that we have been told we are here to fulfil.

Over the years of sharing these learnings with friends around the world, there have been many requests that these teachings be put together in the form of a book. So now we have taken what can be considered as my core messages and put them all together like a ready reckoner which will reliably bring us back home. In the words of an ancient Japanese nun: 'Right here is holy ground, right here I shall build my sanctuary.' May this book be a guide to creating such a sanctuary in our heart of hearts, where peace never departs.

Nandini: Finally, what do you consider a measure of a life well lived?

Nithya: I recommend we each ask ourselves this question deeply. One way to do this is to imagine interviewing ourselves just before we die and asking ourselves what really matters the most. Such reflection can profoundly reorient our priorities and give us a renewed sense of clarity and vision. In my case, I identified five things that would make my life well lived: deepening wisdom, authentic human connections, learning and sharing my lessons, conscious community which means places and spaces for authentic living, and fearless experimentation. In this way, each of us needs to uncover what for us is a life well lived.

Section 1

Acceptance of What Is

1

Unstrung Beads

You are a receptacle, a cup, a chalice,
a holder of fluid pain and late-night confessions,
a keeper of virtue and of silence,
of domestic duty, of propriety,
of family honour, of maternal pride,
of sacrificial smiles,
of keeping the peace and not counting the cost.
You are full to the brim,
all of you is taken.

You need not keep what you did not choose.
You need not be full of what you do not want.
Let it all fall and scatter like unstrung beads.

You are empty. You are clean.
You are free.

To learn, to build, to dream, to desire.
To love and nourish or to set free.
To walk towards or to walk away.

Turn yourself inside out.
Fill yourself with you.

Unburdening

Liberation is hiding in plain sight

In our life we tend to accumulate things—impressions, worries, ideas. Our education too is often about gathering ideas, concepts, ideas of others, quotes, formulae and historical facts but there is almost no emphasis on putting things down.

The Sanskrit saying *'Adya Roopa Upavada Naya'* means that the teacher introduces a concept. That concept creates an experience. Now the teacher takes away the concept. The student is left with the pure experience. In other words, the only purpose of the concept was to lead one to an experience. Unburdening is the process where we put things down, let go of all concepts and ideas, and let go of our stories.

There is a very telling anecdote about the Laughing Buddha.

He was a Zen monk, who lived in China about a thousand years ago and he was well known for being jovial and light-hearted. He wandered from place to place and carried a big sack of goodies and treats of all kinds. He would stop on the wayside and children would come running to him. He would reach into his sack and give each of them a little gift, much to their delight. In a way, he created informal kindergarten schools wherever he went. He would laugh with the children, tell them stories and even roll in the mud with them.

A Zen scholar who saw him acting this way disapprovingly grumbled, 'What kind of behaviour is this?

This is not the way monks are supposed to behave! His clothes are so loose and ill-fitting that they could drop off his body at any time, he carries an enormous bag like a common street seller. He's most un-monk-like. People like him are misrepresenting the true teachings.'

One day, he decided to confront him. As the monk was walking down the road, the Zen scholar blocked his path, pulled out a sword and shouted, 'Tell me the meaning of Zen!' The Laughing Buddha as he was called, suddenly stopped smiling. He released the big bag he was carrying with a loud thud and then he smiled again.

The scholar was not impressed. He challenged him with another question, 'How does one realize Zen?' Now the Laughing Buddha picked up the bag and put it on his shoulder, turned around and started walking away. The scholar realized he was in the presence of greatness and that he had made a grave mistake. He threw his sword away and asked for forgiveness.

In this story, without saying a word, the monk conveyed some of the deepest spiritual truths. What is the meaning of Zen? Put down the burden. What burdens are we carrying? Mental and emotional burdens from the past and worries about the future. If we have willingly picked up those burdens, we can also spontaneously put them down. Once we have learned to put them down, we can re-engage, this time without being caught up in our stories. We don't run away from our responsibilities; we engage, without getting entangled in them. This is why he picked up the bag again and he began walking.

In this way, this monk who on the surface appeared to be jovial and superficial was actually deeply wise. That depth of wisdom did not take away his playfulness. We can be deeply connected to ourselves, and we can also live our lives joyously and with childlike abandon.

This is a light-hearted approach to a really wise way of living. The Laughing Buddha embodies that wonderful teaching. In our daily lives, how do we unburden? There are many ways to do this.

A few tested methods are:

Speaking aloud: The act of saying something aloud seems to clarify, purify and liberate us from our burdens.

Tapping: When I was a monk, in 2006 I came across this method called Emotional Freedom Technique (EFT). In this process you tap various acupressure points and as you tap them, you say whatever is going on for you. It seems to accelerate the process of unburdening.

In the tapping tradition, they ask you to start with sixty days of continuous practice. It is called the Personal Peace Procedure. Write down all the areas of your life, all the memories which you don't feel fully clear about and which creates some contraction within you. Over the next sixty days spend some time everyday just tapping. For example, if you were bullied as a child, the moment you are reminded of that, start tapping. In my experience, the average person has anywhere from two to four hundred unprocessed memories or issues that they carry—that is such a lot of baggage![1]

Meditation: In the Vipassana tradition, it is said one hour of meditation in the morning and one hour in the evening is simply maintenance; this keeps your mind clear.

The Healing Walk: Walking is a great practice of unburdening. When moving our hands and legs, the idea is being in the present or being attentive to the inner process. In the beginning when we walk, we are aware of the layers of unwanted things that come up.

At some point we change focus on our dreams, goals and aspirations, and a different spring comes into our step, and possibilities begin to emerge.

The third stage is even deeper. We envision how it would feel if it is already so and we walk with that energy. As it gets integrated within us, we can examine what it is like to be fully in the present.

Perhaps you will recognize that all our thoughts and worries are dream imaginations. Our preoccupations with when something will happen, how it will happen. But in moments of clarity, we are aware that we are already living the dream, this is it. We have waited our whole life for this moment. Finally, we tune into the awareness of who is even having this experience and we start waking up.

The idea is that no matter which practice we choose, the intention is of unburdening, or else the mind can be scattered and fragmented. The intention is: let this practice open me up—physically, mentally, emotionally. At some point, this unburdening becomes the most fun thing in the world. There is a desire to unwrap ourselves of every concept we have ever known and every stress we have ever known. There is a particular taste to it, it is called *Vishudhi Rasa*—the taste of purification. No other taste in this world can match this taste, and layer by layer by layer things keep coming up and we say bring it on, bring it on, bring it on!

What we welcome is never a problem in this world. What is left is just pure inspiration, pure love, pure attentiveness, pure responsiveness, no reaction, just response, just spontaneous flow! Because all the other layers have gone now, there is no awkwardness anymore.

It is really important that in our own way, in a way that suits us, we create a practice of unburdening. It is just not something to be done once in a while, but something that becomes a daily practice. Through unburdening, we create space. It is said, 'You can never get enough of what doesn't satisfy you.'

The Buddha says that every field of knowledge goes on expanding outwards (like Physics, Mathematics or Origami). This particular field, however, has a conclusion, which is coming back to the source, to the centre. So, ask yourself: who am I at zero distance?

The Buddha says that if one wants to pursue a path, this is a good path. Outwardly we can continue fulfilling our responsibilities, but know very clearly there is no end to that. However, within that, if we introduce unburdening, where we look at our career, family, responsibilities as an opportunity to unburden, right there we have found liberation. Liberation is hiding in plain sight.

Layer by layer, all the fears and aspirations of humanity will arise and be resolved within us. We will journey through life with a lot of blessings, a lot of support. We simply need to tune in. Imagine that our ancestors are looking over our shoulders and smiling and saying, 'Finally this one has got it!' They are saying, 'Infinite blessings, little one, we are with you!' The entire lineage of your ancestors, which is the entire universe, is with you.

So now unburden, unburden, unburden!

Practice: The Four-Minute Meditation

Life can get rather busy at times. The hectic speed and demands we face on a daily basis often leave us feeling stressed, distracted, tired and unhappy. Meditation is an effective way to calm our busy mind, relax our body, be more grounded and find inner peace amidst the chaos of day-to-day life.

Newcomers to meditation often feel intimidated. They imagine a monk sitting in lotus pose for hours on end atop a mountain. But the reality is that meditation is much easier and accessible than most people realize. Here is a simple four-part meditation that I have developed over years of practice. I suggest spending between one and fifteen minutes on each part for a four to sixty minute meditation session.

Part 1. Breath

Bring your attention to your breath. Be mindful of the in-breath. Be mindful of the out-breath. Do this in a relaxed way. Whenever the mind wanders, gently bring it back. If it wanders a lot, then count breaths from one to ten and repeat. Just know the breath as breath, not as 'my' breath.

Part 2. Feelings

Now bring your attention to the sensations felt in the body in this moment. Stay with the sensations. They may be pleasant, unpleasant or neutral. Notice what is happening without judgment or evaluation. Notice: desire arises if it is pleasant, aversion arises if it is unpleasant and boredom arises if it is neutral. Remain alert and attentive in all these states. Notice how sensations arise and fade away, only to be replaced by other sensations. Explore each sensation with curiosity and openness. Just know feelings as feelings, not as 'my' feelings.

Part 3. Silence

Now allow the mind to rest in silence. This does not necessarily mean that there are no thoughts. It just means that the mind is not 'hooked' by these thoughts. They freely come and go like clouds in the sky. Remain as the still and quiet background, as sky-like awareness.

Part 4. *Loving Kindness*

Now practice loving kindness. Radiate loving wishes towards yourself, towards others and even towards those far away, gradually including all sentient beings. Don't try to generate any special feelings. Keep the intention of loving kindness alive in your heart and let feelings come and go by themselves.

When you are ready to end your practice, slowly bring your conscious attention back to your surroundings. Acknowledge your presence in the space around you. Gently wiggle your fingers and toes. Begin to move your hands, feet, arms and legs.

Say silently to yourself:

May I be a channel of blessings for someone today.

May I be a clear channel of beautiful blessings for someone today.

May I be the clearest possible channel of the highest possible blessings, the fastest possible blessings, the purest possible blessings in the world.

And so it is!

Feel each word as profoundly as possible, allowing it to sink into your deeper mind. Open your eyes. Move slowly and take your time getting up. Appreciate yourself and your practice.

Consistency is more important than quantity. Meditating for four minutes every day will reward you with far greater benefits than meditating for two hours, one day a week.

Most beginners find it easier to meditate in a quiet space at home, but as you become more comfortable, begin exploring new places to practice. Meditating outdoors in nature can be very peaceful, and taking the opportunity to meditate on the bus or in your office chair can be an excellent stress reliever.

Begin meditating today!

2

Boundless

To thread a storm,
through the eye of a needle,
to feel the mud, cake beneath my fingernails,
to sing my song, even to empty walls,
to listen to the quiet heartbeat of trees,

to weep and rage, until the heart is spent,
to love, with a quiet ferocity known only to one,
to surrender, without guile, without compulsion,
to share, of abundance and of dearth,
to dance, lost in the body, to time
to sleep, again a seed, in wait for the sun,

to know, I am both fractured and whole,
filled with words and still with silence,
with learning, unlearning, wonder,
and see, that I too, like the weeds,
like the breeze, like the lark, like the rain,
I do not need permission to be.

Shadows, clouds and sky
I am in all, I am in none.

Tell a Better Story

Every Perspective Is Valid, Yet Limited

This is a true story of a young man who grew up in poverty and lived on the streets. He ended up joining a gang and one of the initiation rituals was to get a new member to commit a heinous crime to prove their allegiance and readiness. So, he was asked to murder someone at random and he went and shot a teenager. Not long after, he was apprehended and through his trial, the mother of that teenage boy quietly sat in the stands and did not say a word. He was convicted but since he was underage, he was sentenced to only a few years in prison. As he was being led away, the mother stood up, looked into his eyes and said, 'I am going to kill you.'

A few years passed and this mother decided to visit him while he was incarcerated. They met, had a brief conversation and she left. Few months later she visited again. Over time, a connection formed between them. She would sometimes bring him a cake, check if he needed something, or leave him some stationery.

As the time for his release drew nearer, she asked him what he planned to do once he was free. He said, 'I don't know. I am confused, I don't know what to do.' She said a friend of hers owned a small business and she could possibly get him a job there. She spoke to the prison warden and he said it was possible. The next time they met, she asked him where he planned to live, now that she had arranged a job for him. Again, he said, 'I don't know. I don't have a place to stay.' At this she said, 'You know what, I have a spare bedroom in my house. Until you settle, come and stay with me.' So, when he left the prison, he stayed in her house, shared the food in her home, and went to work at a place she set up for him.

One day she called him to come sit by her. She quietly looked at him for a long time and asked, 'Do you remember what I said to you the day you were convicted?' He replied, 'Ma'am, I can never forget that. You said you would kill me.' She said, 'I have done that. I said I was going to kill the boy who killed my boy and I have done that. Today you are a different person. I have something to ask of you; my son is no longer with us and I have a spare bedroom, would you like to continue staying with me? I would like to adopt you.'

The mother focused on something nobody had seen in that boy. What we focus on expands, and so in ourselves and in others, when we see the best, we bring forth the best. She created a better story.

Every thought is false, but some thoughts are less false. A simple analogy would be—the map is not the terrain. The map is not false but it is not the terrain. Some maps are less false than others in that they may be a little closer representation of the terrain. Eventually though, we have to discard all maps.

What we want to do along the way is to keep updating our software, keep updating our map and keep telling a better story. A story that is a closer representation of what is, even though, at some level, it is always essentially false.

There is an insightful teaching which says, 'What the thinker thinks, the prover proves.' The world appears the way we look at it. Simplistically, if you put on red glasses, it appears red. Put on blue glasses, it appears blue. So, the idea is that we are always looking through a particular lens, a particular kind of filter, and we convince ourselves that it is true.

This brings us to the idea that knowledge is a point of view, and wisdom is a viewing point. Wisdom is not limited to one point of view. Wisdom allows us to view things from many perspectives and that gives us a holistic understanding of what is really going on. Max Müller, the German scholar, famously observed, 'He who knows one, knows none.'

If we only look at things from one culture, one perspective, one language, one way of seeing things, we don't really know it. I once met a professor of political science in Korea. He said, 'Every day I examine twelve newspapers from around the world. I marvel at how the same news is covered so differently by each.' He would quip, 'If you don't read the news you are uninformed, but if you do read the news, you are misinformed.' In other words, after seeing an event from twelve diverse points of view, he had some vague semblance of what was actually going on, since each newspaper has its own agenda.

So, this brings us to a novel concept: Grain of Truth.

There's a grain of truth in what everybody says or does. There is some truth in everything. Even if a person you bitterly dislike says something you completely disagree with, you have to challenge yourself; there's a grain of truth there. Anything anyone says about you, there's a grain of truth there. That grain of truth can become the foundation upon which a conversation can be had or a relationship built.

Ken Wilber is known as one of the most influential thinkers and philosophers of current times. What's fascinating is that he was trying to create a theory of everything. He looked at diverse subjects and ways of looking at life and explored the idea that there is some grain of truth to every single perspective. For example, archaeology sees the world a certain way, cosmology sees the world a certain way, spirituality sees the world a certain way and ecology sees it a certain way; all of these fields see the world in specific ways. Yet, there has to be a grain of truth in all of them.

The question is: how do you bring all of this together?

He came up with a very influential model called the All Quadrants All Levels (AQAL) model.[2] It has four quadrants—I, We, It and Its. Essentially it states that moment to moment, every reality and every phenomenon in it, has four dimensions – Inside, Outside, the Singular and the Plural form.

For example, the **Individual Internal** quadrant corresponds to Consciousness, which could include worldviews, values, purpose and knowledge and the **Individual External** corresponds to Behaviour which includes habits, skills, communication and health. The **Internal Collective** quadrant corresponds to Culture which includes shared values, purpose, societal norms and history and finally, the **External Collective** to

Systems under which fall structure, processes, agreements and metrics.

The framework essentially ties together all these different modes of thinking and every single one of them has some truth to it. This is an incredibly rich and inclusive way to deepen our understanding of everything.

Interestingly, in Jainism the ability to see multiplicity is called *Anekantavada*, or 'non one-sided' doctrine, which means that the ultimate reality is complex and has many aspects, with each one holding some truth in it. Each one of them is internally consistent. This is a powerful contemplation because then the perspective shifts from the ego which wants to assert dominance and say, 'My truth is the only truth, my way is the only way.' Instead, it can now imagine, 'If I had grown up like that, if I had been conditioned like that, if I had those experiences, then I too would think like that.'

Whether you are attached to a spiritual, cultural, collective, or a systems point of view, or any combination of those points of view, it is important to realize that it is just a point of view.

So, if we think of these limitless points of view as data, we can then distinguish data from *the awareness that knows data.* This something that knows is also known as *Rigpa,* which is sky-like open intelligence.

Our work then is to keep distinguishing the data, the concepts, the ideas, from the awareness that knows them. This is of great benefit in our journey towards clarity. You can have a story, you can have a point of view. Once we learn to look at a thought as a map, not as the actual terrain, then we can say this is a truth . . . it is not 'The Truth!'

This awareness leads us naturally to empathy, to understanding, to compassion. This is how we ultimately grow beyond our little individual selves to experiencing life from multiple perspectives. It could be from the perspective of our partner, from the perspective of a child or even from the perspective of a flower.

So, remember the principle of the grain of truth and the fact that everything has some truth to it. There's a beautiful book called *A Course in Miracles*,[3] which says, 'Nothing real can be threatened. Nothing unreal exists. Herein lies the peace of God.'

So right here, in this particular chapter, you will find multiple points of view. We began by saying no thought is real but some thoughts are closer to the real and we are ending it by saying that nothing unreal exists. So right here we see, multiple points of view that at one level seem contradictory and on another, perhaps as Ken Wilber postulates in his works, they're all pointing to some deeper underlying truth. Perhaps that is the path, which begins with confusion.

A simple yet profound way to look at enlightenment is: Great Faith, Great Doubt, Great Awakening.

So how does this connect to our everyday lives? Simply in the awareness that the quality of our life is the quality of the stories we tell. Can we move from a more contracted story to a more expansive one? Can we transcend and include? Can we transcend and include all *previous* stories? Can we transcend all *possible* stories?

As we say, *Yathaa drishtihi thathaa srishtihi,* which means, when we change the way we look at things, the things we look at change. Our perspectives determine the way the world appears to us, both inside and out, individually as well as collectively.

Can we tell a better story?

Practice: Deep Listening

Walk out and find anything. It could be a living or non-living thing. Just look at it with affection. For example, a pillar, a tree, a blade of grass and say to it, 'I see you. I hear you. I feel you. I love you. I am you. Thank you.'

Stay with this object, this thing, for about ten minutes and ask it any question that's in your heart. It could be a struggle you have with your teenager, it could be your business which has failed, or some general advice you want in life. What you may be surprised to find is that you will get something that is very precise.

In other words, everything is speaking to us, but are we listening?

A useful tool is 'Cancel Cancel'; Whenever you have a low quality thought such as 'I can't do that' or, 'How is it going to happen?' just say 'Cancel Cancel'. Don't argue with it, just cancel it. And then you replace it with—'How wonderful!'

Keep welcoming whatever happens. This can be a powerful way to change the stories we tell ourselves even before the unfolding of an action. This is a reminder that we don't have to believe our own limiting stories about ourselves. All we have to do is question them and hold them lightly.

3

Awaken

To slip,
underneath the doors of time,
and fall, through space,
this cage escape,
and find,
there is no dreamer, no dream
and none is as what it seems,
a void, from which, it all has sprung,
you can't outrun, time,
there are no cracks, underneath the door,
the door does not exist.

Dehypnotize Yourself

Be here, now

*Dukh mein sumiran sabh kare, sukh mein kare na koi. Jo sukh
mein sumiran kare, dukh kaahe ko hoye.*—Sant Kabir

*In sorrow everyone remembers the divine, in joy, no one
does. For the one who remembers the divine in joy, how can
sorrow come?*

In my time as a monk, I trained in the tradition of Ajahn Chah, a respected teacher of the Buddhadhamma and a founder of two major monasteries in the Thai Forest Tradition. He was known for his unconventional style of teaching. Sometimes he would walk around the monastery asking an unusual question. In the way that most people greet each other by saying, 'How do you do?', Ajahn Chah would walk around asking, 'How are you suffering today?' He was aware that at some level, we are all suffering, no matter how put together we may seem on the outside. We are struggling, we are striving. There is something in all of us which remains unaddressed, so he would ask, 'How are you suffering today?' Some of the monks would actually say, 'Yes, I am. Today I really am suffering.' In response, he would say, 'You must be holding on to something. Step over here. Step over here where it is always cool.'

Where is here?

Here is simply here, the present. The word present, of course, means now, and it also means a gift. When you see the now as a gift, there is a shift. So *Sumiran,* the remembrance, can serve us well. It means we remember to be present, and sense the obvious or hidden gifts in all happenings. This means that no matter what is going on in our life, we practise saying, 'Thank You, Thank You, Thank You.' Or the Japanese version, '*Arigato, Arigato, Arigato.*' If we assume that life is a curriculum, and no matter how we are tested, we can wake up and grow by getting fully present and saying: Thank You, Thank You, Thank You.

Look for the micro-sufferings throughout the day, the micro-judgments, the micro-irritations, the micro-confusions and just say, 'Thank You.' They have come into your awareness for a reason. It is like they are saying, 'Can you now, at last acknowledge us and love us for who we really are?' Now you say from your heart, 'Thank You, Thank You, Thank You.'

Sometimes people wonder about the idea of enlightenment or nirvana. The whole ending-of-suffering business seems somewhere far off into the future and quite unlikely. Indeed, it can appear that way. Yet the reality is, it is always already here! It is accessible right now. Let me give you a taste of this tasteless state.

Let's do an experiment. For the next fifteen seconds, empty yourself of all desires. Do this now to the best of your ability. Then read on.

Great! In these fifteen seconds, you might have had a micro moment where you truly and genuinely emptied yourself of every possible want, preference, comparison and desire. Believe it or not, you had a mini nirvana right here. It may not seem like much, however, something very significant just happened. You tasted the tasteless taste of your essence which is forever unaffected by the ups and downs of your life. It is like space where nothing sticks, where everything is honoured and held for what it is.

Now when you get back to your wants and desires there is a difference. The wantings will not become hauntings. There is a foundation of ease and trust and flow. You approach all of life with childlike zest and a playful attitude. You do your best and take a rest. You are no longer so hung up and upset when things don't go as planned. There is a broader trust in the completeness of life.

So, there are micro-sufferings and there are micro-nirvanas. We don't have to wait until big upheavals happen in our life. Whatever is happening in life, that is exactly what needs to happen. There are too many people who feel guilty for even the good times in their lives. It is strangely common. When things are going well, they feel guilty about it. Of course, when things are going badly, they are miserable.

A lady once told me that for the last three years things had been going really well. Work was great, she was in a fulfilling relationship, she had a lovely home. And she was petrified! I asked her why. She said that most of her life had been filled with strife and disappointments so she couldn't help wondering when this good phase was going to end. This illustrates an important principle of life: to the extent we have not made peace with our past, we will be unsettled, as we will keep projecting it into the present and future. No matter how good things get, we will be fixated on losing what we have. We will have a survivor's mindset, not a thriver's mindset. So, no matter what's going on, let us be in a state of *Sumiran*, Thank You, Thank You, Thank You! *Arigato, Arigato, Arigato!*

Whatever is coming up in your life, you can ask yourself this: How are you suffering today? And in many instances, perhaps the answer will be, 'Yes, I am suffering.' But, then you have the opportunity to simply respond with gratitude.

Right where there is suffering, right there is freedom. In other words, at the exact place where there is resistance and holding tight, there is the possibility of flow and letting go. So, one way to dehypnotize ourselves is by not being so tightly identified with our suffering and to be in a state of acceptance and gratitude. Simply keep this in your heart—*Micro-Sufferings, Micro-Liberations*.

Another powerful idea to see through our self-deceptions is to be aware of the difference between projection and reflection. Projection is when we add a layer of ideas and opinions to whatever is happening in our life. This often happens without us even realizing the subtle distortions created by projection.

Every moment of your life converges into you at the centre of the universe at all times. The centre of the universe is you. It converges back to you. So, in a way we could say, it is also projected out of you. Every moment of every experience, no matter what age you are or where you are, converges into you, and then, like a projector, gets projected out of you. So, in a way, we are all reacting to our own projections. This is the way some of us are going to live all our life—consistently projecting outwards.

But there is another way. We can choose a life of reflection. Reflection is realizing that everything is just reflecting you. There is no other person out there. It is all a reflection of you. So, what you're reacting to is also you. What you're judging is also you.

As a teenager, I came across a teaching that said whatever quality I see in anyone is in my own self as well. I found this ridiculous. I would think: 'Hey! I don't have that quality.' But now, when I slow down and really examine myself carefully, I say: 'Is it really true that I don't have that quality?' If I am honest, I'd have to admit that in some way, shape or form, I actually do have that quality. Somewhere in me, it exists. At some level, all the so-called positive and the so-called negative qualities are in me. So, reflection essentially means that whatever is showing up in our experience, we don't resist it and meet it with acceptance.

Consider a man who has been married for twenty years and has always criticized his wife for being late. He grumbles that she is always half an hour late for just about everything. He frets and fumes as he waits for her each time they have to go anywhere together. If we were to tell him that he has also been consistently late, he would probably vehemently deny this accusation and assert that he is never late! But you see, he has been twenty years late in accepting his wife, in understanding that this is just the way she is!

In this context Ho'oponopono, the Hawaiian practice can work beautifully. Whatever we encounter, we meet it with 100 per cent responsibility and say, 'I'm sorry. Please forgive me. Thank you. I love you.' This is far from resistance. Resistance is: Why am I like this? Why are you like this? Why is life like this? This and all the other thoughts that lead from there—the 'wouldn't be happening, couldn't be happening, shouldn't be happening' kind of thoughts. So, a way to break out of that cycle is to simply be present and respond from a place of openness and welcoming.

It is also wise to not overanalyse situations. Sometimes our thinking is what is keeping us stuck. You contain everything.

You have all the vices and you have all the virtues in the world. Therefore, whichever way it is manifesting now, the wisdom lies in simply accepting it. This is the way it is. In other words, don't resist it. It's going to complete itself and move on. The more you resist, the more entrenched it gets. The more you try to think about it, analyse it, figure it out, the more deeply intertwined it gets.

I have witnessed people come out of deeply challenging situations with this simple teaching—Don't Resist It. Don't believe that there's something wrong with you. It is what it is. Sometimes all it takes is this perspective of non-resistance to start unravelling whatever was keeping you stuck. A powerful practice I learned from the psychologist Henkels Susan Munich is to look directly into my eyes in the mirror and repeat three times: 'Nithya, just for today, what if there is nothing wrong with you?' This simple practice of self-acceptance can dramatically alter the way we look at ourselves and our lives. When people judge us or offer unsolicited opinions, we don't have to believe them. My friend Akancha says, 'When people say something is impossible, they are talking about their limitations, not yours.'

You may still feel so-called negative emotions and self-doubt, but don't resist them. Simply let it all flow and it will complete itself. There is no need to create and hold on to strong ideas of right and wrong, good and bad, because ultimately, nothing is inherently good and evil. These are all constructs. Yes, when undesirable things happen, we go through them and we learn from them and when desired things happen, we learn from those experiences as well. Eventually we transcend both to arrive at a state where these constructs become irrelevant. There is only a sense of acceptance towards what is, and a state of joyful presence.

Gyandev, a dear friend, is a great example of someone who follows his inner guidance very strongly. He allows it to inform all his decisions, no matter how confounding it may seem to others. Once his inner guidance said to him: Start smoking. So, he got hand-rolled cigarettes and started to smoke. A friend, who is a prominent health coach in India said to him, 'You know, Gyandev, this is really bad for you. You really shouldn't be smoking.' I love Gyandev's response. It is a beautiful, simple answer. He said: 'Would you be willing to allow me to be imperfect?' What a powerful question this is, not just to ask of others but also of our own selves: 'Would you be willing to allow me to be imperfect?' Soon enough his inner guidance directed him to stop smoking and just as easily, he did.

Often, in embracing our imperfections, we discover perfection. Undoubtedly there is a perfection that wants to reveal itself through each of us. All we need to do is simply step away from projecting, which is the life of being lost in our stories, and come to reflecting, which is the life of witnessing, meditation and gratitude. Just be in this state and let the remaining momentum of the mind, of the body, of emotions go ahead and unravel themselves. Whatever momentum there is, let it carry on and dissipate on its own. If you can see your inner self at a distance from all these happenings, you will see that in a way, they have nothing to do with you. They are all passing clouds and you are the eternal sky.

The way I see it, this process of conscious living is about pendulating. What I mean by this is that we oscillate between stepping back and stepping in, witnessing and fully feeling. Sometimes we wonder when we will arrive at a stable state. So many experiences, so many highs and lows, so many breakthroughs followed by new confusions. When does this all end? The truth is—it doesn't end. We will access refined states and lose them. Yet, in the process, we will begin to access a certain something 'underneath'. It is something which we cannot get. It is an underlying reality that will 'get us'. Which means that we die to our imaginary, conditioned self and are awakened to our true nature.

We're all in this together and we're all intimately connected. Our fates, our destinies, our choices are woven into each other, far more intimately than we believe. We don't have the full tapestry right now. We don't have the full picture or blueprint. As we grow in awareness, more and more of the blueprint becomes available. From this perspective, you are likely to say: 'Of course, you would do that, of course, she would do that, of course, they would do that. It had to be. It's part of the blueprint.' And suddenly, in this broader acceptance, their blueprint perfectly aligns with your blueprint. It's gears within gears and these interconnecting gears together make a beautiful mechanism.

Another aspect of dehypnotizing yourself: Don't presume to know. The wiser you get, the more uncertain things get. So, get comfortable with not knowing. Isn't it true that the more uncertain things get, the more alive things are? When we have no fixed ideas, that's when we are maximally alive. Anything can happen! When you allow yourself a state where anything could happen, you play in the field of infinite possibilities.

A Practice:

Here is a straightforward practice that can immediately dehypnotize us. It is inspired by the scripture, *Drig Drishya Vivek*.

1. Look at an object in your environment right now. It could be a painting, a tree—any object.
2. Now recognize that it is an object, while you are the subject. In this moment there is a subject–object relationship. You are the experiencer and it is being experienced.
3. Now look at a part of your own body, for example your right leg. Recognize that it is an object and you are the subject. In this moment, you are the experiencer and your right leg is being experienced.
4. Now think of anything, for example a white lotus. Recognize that this thought is now the object and you are the subject. In this moment, you are the experiencer and the thought of a white lotus is being experienced.
5. Now think of yourself—any aspect of you. Recognize that this thought about you is an object and you are the

subject. In this moment, you are the experiencer and your thoughts about you are being experienced.

6. Now here are some powerful dehypnotizing questions: What is the difference between you and this thought about you? What is the difference between life and your story about life? As you get a sense for this, oscillate between being awareness and the object of awareness. Do this several times until you get a clear taste for this. Practise this for a few moments many times a day. You can also ask yourself: 'Who is taking delivery of this experience?'

4

The Solitary Seeker

How vast this universe,
to fill this raging emptiness,
how much to find
should a seeker be lost,
how boundless its beauty
for eyes that rise to see it,
so much in plain sight,
sans price, sans cost

and yet, and yet
we seek worlds in another,
and build for ourselves
these constellations of hope
and fall then to our knees
at our own harsh awakening
and flail about helpless,
bound by our very own rope

while the journey of the self,
no end and no beginning,
is beyond what exists,
within the walls of one heart,
yes, a hand can be held

yes, a mind be well loved,
but the passion of the seeker
courses a solitary chart.

The Power of Attention

The quality of my life is the quality of my attention

Have you seen a geodesic dome? It's a dome with no supporting pillars. It's made of three-dimensional triangular sub-structures that make the dome both strong and stable for its size. It was named and popularized by a visionary architect and inventor named Buckminster Fuller, who was successful, married to a beautiful woman and they had a lovely child; it was a picture-perfect life. Then the unexpected happened, their beloved child died at age four. Fuller was shattered like he had never been before.

One day he went to the Great Lakes, stood on a big rock, took off his clothes and was about to jump because he couldn't bear the pain of having lost his daughter. Just as he was about to jump into the frigid waters, he suddenly felt as though he was suspended several feet above the ground enclosed in a white sphere of light. A voice spoke directly to Fuller, and declared:

'From now on you need never await temporal attestation to your thought. You think the truth. You do not have the right to eliminate yourself. You do not belong to you. You belong to the Universe. Your significance will remain forever obscure to you, but you may assume that you are fulfilling your role if you apply

yourself to converting your experiences to the highest advantage of others.'[4]

At that moment, he stepped away from taking his life, put his clothes back on and went back home. The story goes that for the next few years, he just lived in contemplative silence. He emerged into a flurry of invention, activity and discovery. He invented countless things and has several patents to his name. Not only did he travel all over the world and was granted several honorary doctorates, he served as an inspiration for countless scientists who came after him. He said all his accomplishments were fuelled by his desire to embark on 'an experiment, to find what a single individual could contribute to changing the world and benefiting all humanity'.

His story is a testament to the power of attention applied to an inspiring ideal. As we stay true to our larger, more expansive purpose, the means inevitably follow.

We are often told that time is our most precious resource. Actually, that's not entirely true. When we are more energetic, we accomplish more in the same amount of time. So, energy is a more important resource than time. Even more important than energy is attention, since energy flows where attention goes. This means the most valuable resource is attention.

So, here's a good question for us to ask: How many of us wake up in the morning and say, 'Today, my goal is to spend at least six hours on social media.' Probably, no one. But if you look at your screen time, it's actually around there. How can we reclaim our attention—our most precious resource?

Anything we do with full attention is not a problem. Actually, it's quite enjoyable. As the stoics say: Focus strengthens our core, it makes us resilient. It gives us the strength to know that whatever the future holds, we will be able to face it. If we cannot even face the little ups and downs of our daily life with equanimity, then of course, we will live fearful of the future. However, if we can have some measure of collectedness, that is, if we are able to stay steady of gaze, open to the full experience of life, including opening up our body and our breath, then we can get through anything life brings to us.

Let me tell you a story. Diogenes, a Greek philosopher, was known for his unconventional views and lifestyle. Unlike the other philosophers, he was rustic, foulmouthed and uncouth. He lived on the street and behaved like a tramp. However those who knew him were aware of his wisdom. Diogenes was unabashedly authentic, and he was able to live in that manner because he didn't want anything from anybody.

Alexander the Great heard about Diogenes and was very impressed by the stories about him so he decided to go meet the philosopher. Diogenes was sitting in the sun when Alexander arrived with a retinue of bodyguards. He gave Diogenes an open offer and said, 'I really admire you, ask me for anything, and I will give it to you.' Being the Emperor that he was, he was actually capable of giving Diogenes anything that he asked for. The story goes that Diogenes looked at him and simply said, 'Stand out of my light.'

How is this relevant to us? Nowadays, Alexander the Great is our mobile phone. 'What do you want? Should I book you a ticket? Should I play some music? Do you want a new recipe? You name it, I'll give it to you.' We get sucked in. It looks like it is free. But it is not. You pay with your light, and your light is your attention.

One of the fascinating aspects of meditation is that when you pay attention to a mantra, you pay attention to a sound, or a visualization—it is basically directing your attention. The first step is usually exclusive attention. So, when I say, 'pay attention to the furthest sound you can hear', then by definition you're trying to exclude everything else, you're trying to focus on that furthest sound. Pay attention to the colour red in this room and instantly you've taken out all the other colours.

There was a famous psychology experiment about counting the number of passes during a game of basketball. While this happens, a man in a gorilla suit walks past the frame. Most people are so busy counting that they don't notice him. Exclusive attention! You pay attention to something so deeply that you miss out on everything else. Even for training our attention, this can be helpful. So, the purpose of this type of practice is to stabilize and strengthen our attention muscles.

The next stage is inclusive attention. You include everything. My teacher used to call it 'no place to stand'. So, normally you have a mantra to return to, or the breath to return to or something else to rely on. Yet, as you go along, there comes a point where there is 'no place to stand'.

Every foundation is taken away. Another way of saying this is, 'Return to centre, release the centre.'

When I began this journey, I noticed something very curious. I would sit to meditate—in the beginning, maybe for just ten or fifteen minutes—and my mind would be all over the place. But still, at the end of it, I would feel lighter. When I would open my eyes, something would feel different. Definitely calmer, clearer and more aligned.

I was inspired by one of my teachers in North-East Thailand. Once he spent the annual three-month rains retreat in a remote place. Every day he would walk a long distance through the mud and rain to a village to collect alms. The villagers there were so abjectly poor that all they could offer him was rice and some chilli paste. This is all he ate for three months. Nothing else. I was very moved that my own teacher had been through this predicament and had borne it so patiently. I thought I should try to eat only rice for three days to pay homage.

So, the next day I went on the alms round as usual and received the food the villagers offered me. On my return, I removed all the fruits, vegetables and sweets, and I just had rice left in my bowl. I was expecting a very boring meal. I was surprised to find that every bite I took tasted a little bit different. You see the whole village had given me rice and so each family had used slightly different rice and had prepared it in their own way. I was amazed to find a world of flavour in each bite. When I would normally eat, there would be a bite in my mouth and I would be planning my next bite. So, I was actually not fully attentive to this bite.

My eyes would track what I wanted to eat next and in what combination. In this process, I would not fully appreciate the morsel in my mouth, no matter how tasty it was. I was not really present.

Yet on this day, there was only rice in my bowl. So, there was no great urgency to plan my next bite. I relaxed. I was amazed to find that it was a calm, slow and meditative meal. And not only did I feel physically nourished, I felt spiritually nourished by that meal. What I expected would be a difficult, boring and unpleasant experience turned out to be one of the most fulfilling meals I ever had. In those three days of eating nothing but plain rice, I realized the real pleasure came not from the quality and variety of food, it came from the quality and singularity of attention.

My teacher used to say, one of the hardest places to practice mindfulness is while eating. You can be a monk for years and you'll still struggle to be mindful while eating. In fact, during the habitual parts of our life, for example, bathing or brushing our teeth, we tend to go on autopilot and lose mindfulness. To be aware while eating is a very advanced practice. Our teachers would say, 'Don't be hard on yourself, it can take time.' To have even one meal, from beginning to end, without losing mindfulness can take years of practice.

The quality of my life is the quality of my attention.

I had taken a group to Bhutan some years back. It is a beautiful country. At one point, our bus stopped for a break and we all got off. The view of the mountain range from there was absolutely breathtaking! When I looked around, I noticed everyone immediately started taking and posing for photographs and selfies. Then they compared photos and began dispersing. Is that it?

Had we come all this way after driving for hours only to take a few photographs? I invited everyone to put aside their phones and cameras, and simply sit there for twenty minutes, gazing at the mountains and taking in the moment. Until that moment, none of us had actually connected with the mountains. We did not take in the mountains, the cameras did. So, we all sat there and just observed. It was such a delicious experience. I sense, in some way the silence and the majesty of those mountains came alive and became a part of us forever.

If we go through our lives, trying to grasp at moments, they slip out of our fingers. Instead, when we slow down, breathe and connect, we find everything is already a part of us.

A Practice:

Notice the kind of sounds you are hearing—some are louder, some are softer. What is the most subtle or distant sound you can hear? And what is the loudest, most obvious sound you can hear? Every sound gets you deeper into your own clarity, deeper into your awareness. Now, instead of imagining yourself as a body, just see yourself as space and within this space, of course, there are sounds. There's also a sensation of breath. So, instead of a feeling that you are watching the breath, have a sense that the breath is coming and going within the space. You are the unmoving space within which different kinds of activities, thoughts and memories are all arising. It is like you are the screen on which the movie of this moment is being projected. Normally we identify with the content of the movie. But at this moment, can you recognize yourself as the screen? As the unmoving background on which all of this comes and goes. If you can recognize that for even a microsecond, that is the beginning of awakening.

5

The Dance

To love is to meet more than breath,
its rise and fall,
to meet,
the cadence of each day,
to lead, allow to be led
and pause, with pause,
rest, with rest
and be so very silent,
to hear the whisper of a song in a beloved's heart
and meet,
dance, with dance.

Joy beyond Self-Interest

Practicing Mudita

At one of my retreats, an attendee shared, 'Nithya, I was working in an IT company. My friend and I were scheduled to be sent abroad. It had been in the works for almost two years. One day my friend came in and said that he had been selected for an offshore project. Right away I was so happy for him and said, "This is fantastic news. I am so happy for you. Let's go celebrate."'

'Many years later, my friend told me that he was afraid to tell me that he had been selected since both of us were in line for the same thing. He feared it could impact our friendship. However, when he saw that I was genuinely happy for him, he realized that I was more than just an office colleague; I was a true friend.'

That feeling is called *Mudita*.

The four *Brahmaviharas* are sublime attitudes that can be cultivated boundlessly. They are: Loving Kindness or *Maitri*, Compassion or *Karuna*, Appreciative Joy or *Mudita* and Equanimity or *Upeksha*. *Mudita* is one of the most fun Brahmaviharas of all. One of my teachers used to call it 'the lazy person's way to enlightenment'. It's because all you have to do to practise *Mudita* is to rejoice wholeheartedly in the happiness, success and good fortune of others. You can simply think of people who have good fortune and say, 'How wonderful!'

Mudita is the wish 'may you not be separated from your good fortune.' To understand it better, let's look at the opposite of *Mudita*. This is where the comparative mindset could come up. I remember, as a child, I was very happy when my mother gave me a digital watch I had longed for. For many months, I was joyful, until I realized my friend had an analog watch. I thought, 'Wow, he's got the one that grown-ups have.' Suddenly I was not happy with my watch anymore. I said, 'Mom, I too want that watch. I have this little childish watch.' So, in an instant, all my prior happiness was gone and I wouldn't let my mother rest until she bought me that watch. In other words, I was doing just fine until I realized that someone else was doing better or had something better.

Let's look at a fun example. Imagine a person who has donated a lot of money to build a big hospital. On the day of the inauguration of the hospital, he is on the stage with all the dignitaries and they are talking about what a great hospital this is going to be. As you are sitting there listening to them, your heart just fills up with an amazing sense of *Mudita*. What an amazing thing this person has done! He has given all of this money, he has spent all his time, all of his efforts, to build this huge hospital. So many people are going to get cured, so many are going to get employed, so many are going to benefit. What a wonderful source of blessings this hospital will be!

It is said that karmically your *punya* (good karma) is no less than the *punya* of the man who actually built the hospital. In fact, chances are yours is even more, because the person who built it sometimes has a bit of an ego. So, it is possible that the person who is delighting in this act is creating even purer karma than the person who built it in the first place.

I am reminded of a book *Maro Up* by Ken Honda.[5] It is essentially the philosophy of Wahei Takeda, also called the 'Warren Buffet of Japan' because of his acumen as an investor. With every chapter of this book, something unlocks inside the heart. More than a book, it is almost like an energetic transmission, because this person has such

different views on life and money than many of us have
been conditioned to have.

The word *Maro* in Japanese means a true heart, a sincere
heart. His whole philosophy is based on increasing your
Maro, since this is the foundation of true success, fortune
and achievement. When your heart is true and sincere,
then the whole world responds accordingly. In his case, he
naturally had this *Maro* quality.

In fact, one of his first business failures also showed his
Maro. He started a factory selling children's confectionery.
He thought everything was going really well, until one day
all the orders stopped, leaving him surprised and confused.
Later, he got to know that the customers had stopped buying
the candies. However, the wholesalers liked him so much
that they kept ordering from him anyway. There came a
point when the stock was just too much and they couldn't
order anymore. This was an example of *Maro*, where they
did business with him because they liked him as a person.
Consequently, Wahei improved on his product because he
felt that people should never suffer on his account.

Wahei's whole life is about *Mudita*. In Japanese, *Arigato*
means thank you. His principle was that whatever comes
into your life, you say 'thank you, thank you, thank you'!
Wahei would gift a gold coin to anyone he met. For him,
gold is not a physical element. It is a spiritual element. How
fascinating! What kind of abundance mentality! His way of
thinking is so unique and seems to run counter to how most
of us have been conditioned, which is to operate largely
from a scarcity mindset.

That is how the principle of *Mudita* works. The underlying benefit of *Mudita* is that whatever you appreciate, will appreciate in your life. If you are appreciating someone's good qualities, someone's success, someone's good fortune, at that moment, you are experiencing it within yourself. You are strengthening it within yourself. You are allowing it for yourself. Whatever you appreciate, you experience more of right now and by resonance, you attract more of into your life.

This reminds me of a story. Once, there were two sadhus meditating in two different parts of the Himalayas. Thirty years had passed. They were meditating on Lord Brahma, seeking a boon from him. Finally, Brahma appeared before one of them and said, 'I am pleased with your devoted practice. I will grant you a boon. Ask for anything.' The hermit replied, 'I want to be liberated from the cycle of birth and death.' Brahma said, 'Certainly it will happen. It will take as many lifetimes as there are leaves on this tree.' The sadhu looked up and thought, 'Oh my goodness! There are so many leaves on this tree. What have I been doing? I have spent thirty years meditating! What a waste of time! Lord Brahma is not as powerful as I had imagined.' He was very upset. He threw away his prayer beads and walked away dejected.

Soon after, Lord Brahma appeared before the second sadhu and asked, 'What do you want, my son? I am pleased with your *tapasya* (penance).' The sadhu said, 'I want to be liberated from the cycle of birth and death.' Brahma gave him the same reply, 'Certainly! It will take as long as there are leaves on this tree—those many lifetimes." The sadhu looked up and saw a similar kind of tree, with as many leaves, and he was thrilled. He said, 'You mean there is a finite number? You mean it is soon going to be over?' He got up and started to dance with joy. 'How wonderful! How wonderful! This cycle of suffering is almost over. How blessed and fortunate am I!' He sat down to meditate and, on the spot, he was liberated!

I am reminded of a more contemporary example. A beggar is sitting with a bowl. In the bowl are a few coins and a sign that reads, 'Please spare change.' On another road in the same city, another man is sitting on the ground. He too has a bowl with a few coins in it, and a sign that says, 'If you need, please take.' Can we even call him a beggar? We would have to call him a king. He has so little and yet he is offering what he has to anyone who needs it.

Mudita really opens up our hearts and instead of feeling narrow and focused on self, it invites us to rejoice in the joy of all. It is about changing the win–lose mentality, i.e., an assumption that if you are winning, then I am losing. With *Mudita*, you turn that around and make it a win–win mentality. Everyone is winning, in their own time, in their own space.

There is a story in the scriptures of Sariputta and Mahamoggalana. The Buddha considered Sariputta as his right-hand disciple and Mahamoggalana as his left-hand disciple. Sariputta was foremost in wisdom and Mahamoggalana was foremost in psychic powers. Once Sariputta was meditating and a demon found it very irritating that this monk with a shiny, shaved head was sitting so calmly. The demon hit Sariputta's head hard. Sariputta was so deep in meditation that the blow did not affect him.

When he emerged from his meditation, Mahamoggalana said, 'How wonderful and marvellous! This big demon came and hit you so hard on the head and you are just fine!' Sariputta said, 'I have a bit of a headache. But, how wonderful and marvellous! I never saw a demon, but you saw a demon! Your psychic powers are so astonishing.'

So, they are both rejoicing. They are practising *Mudita* for each other!

Any good quality that you appreciate in anybody, you cannot help but strengthen it in yourself. You cannot see kindness in others without awakening some kindness in yourself. You cannot appreciate some truthfulness in others without awakening some truthfulness in yourself. You cannot appreciate someone's wonderful spiritual attainment without developing and strengthening it in yourself.

By doing this, we can change the culture of the world. Culture is stories and traditions. The culture of any place is the stories that you hear about what people did when they faced adversity, what they did when they gained prosperity.

So, we are changing the story here. Also, I believe we are changing our mental picture of what society is. This is how we change the culture of our family, change the culture of our world—it is by telling stories. As we practise *Mudita* in our lives, we make the world we inhabit a kinder and more joyous place for all.

A Practice:

1. Think of any unfulfilled aspiration which someone else has achieved. It could be health, wealth or relationships. Fill your heart with *Mudita* for that person. *'Your happiness is my happiness.'*

2. Now think of anything that you wanted to do or experience in your life that someone somewhere has. Fill your heart with intense, immense, boundless *Mudita* towards this person. *'May you have even more of this. I rejoice in your good fortune.'*

3. And now, think of any quality that someone possesses that you don't have. Practice *Anant Mudita*. Infinite Appreciative Joy!

Take three slow breaths integrating these deep into your being. Make an intention: I invite *Mudita* to take up permanent residence in my heart and in my being, whether or not I have practised it before. From this moment forward, *Mudita* is one of the main themes of my life. Everything I do, everything I perceive, everywhere I go, there is the fragrance of *Mudita*. I am discovering this beautiful *Mudita* is a living energy and it is the easiest, most joyful, most fun way back home to my true nature. And so it is. And so it is. And so it is. *Tathaasthu!*

6

Healing

If you have come from brokenness,
you already know what it takes to keep someone safe,
if you have witnessed lives torn apart,
by love or hate,
by debt, by greed, by fate,
you already know what it takes,
to mend the frayed corners of a heart
that has been spent,

if you have hurt someone,
because you could,
because you wanted to,
because they hurt you,
or they could have,
you already have seen your shadows,
faced your own darkness,
and you will understand it,
when you see it in another,

if you have lost,
something, everything,
and been left holding an enormous emptiness,
an unpacifiable rage,

your knees close to your chest,
eyes emptied of tears,
you already know what it means
to have, to love,
a person, a purpose, a life,

and how very fragile it is,
how very fragile it all is
how one ill wind can mean
lives tossed about
without a moment to gather your things,
or say your goodbyes

if you have lived full well,
in the middle of your own life,
you already know more than you imagine,
have more to offer,
than you know you have,
you already know what it takes to heal,
so won't you offer it,
to the world but first, to your own self?

Empowerment through Complete Responsibility

Suffering = Experience × Resistance

The notion of complete responsibility can be unsettling, especially in a world that often makes us feel powerless in many ways. When so much appears out of our control, we can feel resistance against taking responsibility for situations we didn't personally create or perpetuate. I'd like to share the astounding story of Nick Vujicic, a man who embodies the idea of someone who has taken full responsibility for his life.

Nick was born with no hands and legs (due to a rare condition known as Tetra-amelia syndrome). Instead of regarding this as a handicap, his parents decided that he was going to be like any able-bodied child and go to a regular school.

Nick has learned to just about do everything by himself. He can drive a car, he goes swimming, he goes surfing, he plays several musical instruments and he proposed to his wife by slipping on the ring using his mouth. He has found a way around things that you and I would consider difficult. He has three lessons: I choose to be grateful, I choose to dream big and I choose to never give up.

Taking full responsibility for whatever comes up in life is a radical idea because it is life transforming. When we don't take responsibility, we are waiting for the other person to change, or the government to change, or the situation to change, or for the economy to change. So, we are going to be waiting for a very long time!

When we take hundred per cent responsibility, we also become conscious of our response to what is happening. We become aware that we can respond in two significant ways. We could either react through memory, which includes our programming, conditioning, preferences and our judgements. Or, we could respond from a place of clarity and inspiration.

Responding from memory comes from the momentum of the past—our own past and our cultural and ancestral past, or even from the transgenerational trauma of humanity. Responding from inspiration comes from clarity, from freshness, from beingness. How do we meet each moment of our lives? Are we going to meet it with reaction and resistance? Are we going to replay the old ways of looking at it again and again and again, which we know haven't served us? Or are we going to look at it with fresh eyes, the fresh eyes of awareness and wholeheartedness?

There are many paths that lead us to regaining our power. One of the paths can be traced to a spiritual practice from Hawaii called Ho'oponopono, which we have touched upon briefly before. The word translates to 'correction'. Ho'oponopono is about correcting our distorted ways of looking at things. If something is unhealed in the world around us, according to Ho'oponopono, something in us needs healing and correction because we are not separate from the world.

We've seen that in some situations, some people are calm while others get very agitated. The situation in itself is neutral. For example, when it rains, some people get very upset. Somebody says, 'Oh, my picnic got cancelled!' On the other hand, the farmer says that he is so happy he finally got rains for his crops. So, you see that raining by itself is a neutral state, a natural phenomenon. Our thoughts about the situation colour our experiences.

With Ho'oponopono you come to a state of balance. You take full responsibility for what's happening. Sometimes people assume this means they are to blame for all the upheavals in the world. This is not an accurate understanding of this principle. Remember: It isn't my fault, yet it IS my responsibility ('response–ability'). No matter what happens I have the ability to respond in many ways, some skilful and some not so skilful. This is how we need to understand the idea of full responsibility.

To practice Ho'oponopono, we think or say four simple yet powerful statements.

I'm sorry.
Please forgive me.
I love you.
Thank you.

These statements lead to a powerful shift. The idea is that throughout the day, whenever something is bothering you, instead of resisting it, instead of tightening yourself around it, you come back to these statements.

There are four levels of consciousness in Ho'oponopono.

The first is **victimhood**, where you are completely at the mercy of other people, other situations and all kinds of happenings. You are constantly in a state of resistance. We believe, 'Life is happening TO me.'

The second is **empowerment**, where you realize that you are powerful. You clarify your priorities and your broader vision, set goals, take steps towards them and activate the power of *sankalp-shakti* (intention). We believe, 'Life is happening BY me.'

The third level is that of **surrender,** where you recognize that you may not even know what you really want and what is truly best for you in the larger context. How often have you felt certain about a course of action only to discover later that it does not really fulfil you? So, even our convictions in what we want can be unreliable. We cannot be sure that it is not the best for us in the long run. This is why we begin to trust in a larger intelligence of life and surrender by saying, for example, 'May this or something better happen for the highest benefit of all!' This clears the subconscious resistance and attachment that can keep us stuck. We believe, 'Life is happening THROUGH me.'

The fourth stage is **awakening**. This is where the imaginary separation between our self, others and the world is seen as an illusion. There is a sense of oneness. One is in touch with an underlying unity beneath the apparent diversity of the world. In this stage, we feel like 'Life is happening to life.' This is when we are awakened to the dreamlike nature of reality.

The purpose of Ho'oponopono is to move us from victimhood to awakening by taking every single event and happening in our life (no exceptions!) as an opportunity to practise taking hundred per cent 'response-ability', and to clean up through forgiveness, love and gratitude. What makes Ho'oponopono so remarkable is that it can be incorporated seamlessly into our daily lives. The four simple statements have the power to profoundly transform our perspectives from moment to moment. They change our way of looking at the world and empower us to act from inspiration instead of conditioning.

This brings me to a remarkable story. The revered sixth Sikh Guru Hargobind Singh was wrongly imprisoned during Emperor Jahangir's rule in Gwalior. The Guru was such an evolved being, that even in prison, his presence exuded such peace, harmony and love that the energy of the place became similar to that of an ashram. All the other political prisoners would join him every day for devotional singing and a palpable sense of peace and calm pervaded the place.

The story goes that Jahangir's wife started to get nightmares that a holy man had been imprisoned and should be released immediately. She shared her visions with her husband, who dismissed them as inconsequential dreams. However, these were recurring nightmares and she finally told Jahangir that he was inviting calamity upon himself if he didn't pay heed and release the holy man immediately. Finally, Jahangir relented and asked for Guru Hargobind Singh to be released. But the Guru said, 'I don't want to be released until the other innocent people here are also released.' This enraged Jahangir who changed his mind and decided not to release him after all. Meanwhile, his wife's nightmares continued unabated.

Finally, Jahangir came up with a plan. He decreed that Guru Hargobind Singh would be released, and only the prisoners who could hold on to the end of his kurta would be allowed to go with him. Upon hearing this, the prisoners cut his kurta into many long strips and in this way, many more people could hold on to it and were released from prison. The fable goes that his kurta had fifty two corners and he walked out of captivity with fifty two others with him. It is said, one of the reasons the Sikhs celebrate Diwali is because it was on this day that their revered Guru and other prisoners were released. So, you see, Guru Hargobind took full responsibility for his situation, remained undaunted by his predicament and was able to make possible what was seemingly impossible.

Perhaps there are many ways to transform suffering into a force for good. There's a lovely definition of suffering, which comes from Byron Katie, a renowned American teacher and author known for a method of self-inquiry known as 'The Work'. She says, 'When I argue with reality, I lose—but only 100 percent of the time.' [6] When we resist what is happening in our life, that's when we start to suffer. Emotional upheaval is created not by the event itself but by our resistance to it. I have a formula to explain the nature of suffering.

$$Suffering = Experience \times Resistance$$

The more we resist, the more we suffer. The more we accept, welcome and embrace what is happening, the less we suffer. This is a really important principle. Happiness then would be loving what is and suffering is judging what is, resisting what is.

Reaching this stage of zero resistance comes from a place of wisdom. This place lives between stimulus and response. In that gap, our wisdom lives, in the space where we have an opportunity to decide. A lot of the current research on the workings of the brain suggest that what we think of as free will is not really free will. A few moments before we consciously decide to do something, our brain has already decided for us. But we think that we made that decision. Neuroscience has proof that before we think that we decided it, the brain activity has already begun. In this case, are we all then just destined to live like robots?

Actually, no. There was a thought, and yes, there indeed was an impulse. You don't have to follow through. There's a moment where you can check: Is it really helpful? Is it really useful? Should I really do this or not? So that gap is where our wisdom is. That is where we shift from being reactive to being 'response-able'.

What happens when we instantly act upon emotions? We don't feel our emotions or give them time to be, or to play out. This leads to another path to empowerment: fully feeling our feelings and emotions. Our feelings don't want to be fixed. They want to be felt; they want to be given this space to be. So, if we look at emotion as energy in motion, when something happens and it triggers something inside of us, can we just allow this energy to remain in motion and not create a story around it? Stories that we tell ourselves again and again: 'I'm like this, they're like this, the world is like this . . .' These thoughts keep us stuck. Just for a moment, let us mimic children who wholeheartedly feel every emotion. And guess what? A few minutes later, in the way of children, we are fine. We would have forgotten about it and moved on. How? It's because we have not created a big story around it.

A good way to understand emotion is to think of it as energy in motion. When we are upset, it is like our energy is stuck and constipated. That is why it feels so unpleasant. Energy wants to be in motion. Some of the most effective therapies for releasing trauma these days are what are known as somatic therapies. Instead of just talking about your problem, therapists ask you: 'When you think that or when you say that, what happens in your body? Can you be with the feeling? Where are you feeling it? What's happening now?' The intent is to fully feel what you are feeling and wherever you feel a contraction or a heaviness, ask: 'Can I relax and allow this to flow?' For instance, when I feel a heaviness in my heart, I directly tune into that feeling and say: 'Relax and flow . . . relax and flow, where do you want to go? Relax and flow, where do you want to go?' It is fascinating! Energy wants to move; energy wants to flow. All you need to do is to gently allow it.

So, taking full responsibility also means allowing ourselves to fully feel what we are feeling. This is where the emotional alchemy begins. This is where real transformation begins.

A Practice:

A teacher and life coach named Tom Stone came up with a method called CORE, or Centre of Remaining Energy.

He found that whatever you're feeling, you can come to the centre of that.

You could try it right now. Whatever it is that you're feeling right now, can you come to the heart of that and really feel it? And then stay with it for ten seconds or fifteen seconds. Close your eyes and fully feel whatever you are feeling right now. Now notice what the prominent feeling is and locate it in the body. Allow yourself to feel it instead of resisting it. Can you allow it? Can you give it space to be? Give it the space to breathe? If you can identify something that you're feeling, then come to the very centre of that. It doesn't have to be unpleasant, it could be a pleasant feeling. Come to the very centre of that. Relax and flow. Relax and flow. Relax and flow, where do you want to go? Come to the centre of what's happening now. The centre may have shifted, so check for that. As you breathe and tap into whatever you're feeling, fully feeling your feelings, come into the CORE, the centre of remaining energy. Of course, your mind will wander. So, bring it back and breathe with and into whatever you are feeling. Take a deep breath. And you can slowly open your eyes.

It's a beautiful practice that gives us a small taste of what it is like to fully feel a feeling.

7

Prayer

I stripped the bangles off my wrists,
the words came off my tongue,
no lamps, no bells, no soft incense,
no beating of the drum

I came without a need, desire
a wanting of my heart,
I came without a reason, end
I came without a start

The earth, the sky, the sun, the moon,
they spoke to me of You,
I saw You where the eagles soared,
they whispered of You too

and You saw then the prayer in me,
which I had now become,
and You then smiled and simply said,
my child to me has come.

The Beauty of No Agenda

Be like melting snow. Wash yourself of yourself

—Rumi

Once, when I was in Mexico, the guest house I was staying at had a wall in the kitchen where travellers could write something memorable. I remember a quote that said, 'Sometimes when we lose our way, we find ourselves.' Isn't this true? We may find that when we venture away from our tight plans, life unfolds in wonderfully unexpected ways.

Many years ago, I took a group of people to Bodh Gaya, the place where the Buddha attained enlightenment, and to some of the surrounding places which were of spiritual and historical significance. One day, a member of the group invited us to his village nearby. This was not part of our itinerary; however, he was so genuine and so sincere that we said, 'Alright, let's do this.' So, he called ahead and informed his village. There were thirty of us in a large bus and as we got off the main highway and onto a bumpy road, all of us were wondering what we were getting ourselves into.

As we reached, we saw that the entire village was waiting to welcome us. They had erected a large *shamiana* (a tent put up typically for ceremonies like marriages). They lovingly served us lunch and showed us around the village. We spent a few hours there and before we returned, they also offered us some local delicacies which one wouldn't easily have access to in the cities. So, at the end of the trip, when asked about highlights, for many it was this visit to the village, something that wasn't part of our original plan. We had taken a risk, tried something different and that became the most memorable part of the trip. This is the beauty of no agenda.

Almost all of us have an agenda in mind through most of our day, as well as invisible antennae which sense the agenda other people come with. In some, this awareness is slightly developed and in others, highly intuitive. At the very least, as we are walking down the street and are approached by someone, most of us can sense if it is to sell us something, ask us for directions or an attempt to convert us to a different religion. In some, this sense is so refined that each time we are with someone, we can sense their underlying motive. Of course, some of us may overdo it. We may believe everybody has an agenda or a vested interest, and even if people approach us with good intentions, we may mistrust them.

In a documentary on an enlightened sage named Nisargadatta Maharaj,[7] Jack Kornfield said, 'Part of what made it so extraordinary to be with Nisargadatta was to be with someone who wanted nothing from you. I've never in my life been with someone who wanted less from me or anybody. And in that not wanting anything, there was a sense of tremendous freedom and tremendous love.'

When I was living as a Buddhist monk in the forests of Thailand and Sri Lanka, one of the things they taught us was to not plan what we were going to say in a Dharma talk. Can you trust that you will know what you have to say in the moment when you have to say it? The idea is that in this way even you will learn something. So, what they taught us is that instead of preparing your speech, could we prepare our heart? Instead of preparing our content, can we prepare our consciousness?

Jacob Liberman is an author I enjoy very much. He is also a scientist who studied the eye and light very deeply. In his book *Wisdom From an Empty Mind*,[8] he talks about an occasion when he was to give a lecture on a subject he was well known for. Yet, as the host was introducing him, it struck him that he had prepared every line of the speech on a subject he was supposed to be an internationally acclaimed expert on. He realized that his whole life had been a series of rehearsed announcements. This hit him so hard that his hand quivered and all his index cards fell to the ground. Instead of picking them up, he just stepped on to the podium and shared what he had just experienced.

The entire group sighed in collective relief as they felt they had been spared a rehearsed lecture. He then went on to speak from the heart and instead of the scheduled one-hour, it turned into a three-hour interaction and nobody wanted to leave. It just goes to show, it takes endless practice and preparation to be who you are not, and it takes no preparation to be who you are. If you are really comfortable with who you are, you do not need to prepare. You can just show up and share your gifts. We all have gifts. When you really show up and share your gifts and you synergize with others' gifts, that's when magic happens!

It takes courage to show up. Ajahn Sumedho, one of my teachers, had worked in the navy. He later got interested in Zen and practised in America. Eventually, he came to Thailand and was ordained as a Buddhist monk with our teacher Ajahn Chah, who had a way of challenging his students. On one of the festival nights where thousands of people had come, Ajahn Chah finished his discourse and asked Ajahn Sumedho to speak.

Ajahn Sumedho mentioned that he hardly knew any Thai; however, Ajahn Chah insisted that he speak. So, he put together all his Thai vocabulary and somehow managed to give a discourse for half an hour. At the point when he felt he was done, Ajahn Chah said, 'Keep going.' So, he kept going and somehow, he kept it together for one more hour. Again, Ajahn Chah said, 'Keep going.' By now most of the audience were walking away and he was repeating himself as he only knew a smattering of Thai words. In this way, two hours passed, and by the third hour, only a few old ladies were still seated, and some had already fallen asleep.

Ajahn Sumedho said that towards the end of those three hours, he had touched the lowest ebb of audience response and yet his teacher continued to make him speak. He said that was the day he lost the fear of worrying about what people think of him when he speaks. That literally liberated him. He called it 'Being Hootless,' which means you don't give a hoot. That requires a deep self-integration.

In the early days when I was teaching, I would write an intention for what could be the best possible outcome for any gathering. Then I would note a few themes or practices I felt were appropriate. Things would invariably match the intention, sometimes in uncanny and remarkable ways. As this went along, I began to wonder if I could ever really know the best possible outcome in any situation. For instance, it might be possible that someone would be disappointed in my teachings and thereby begin to rely more on their inner guidance. This inspired me to come empty and agendaless to my talks and retreats, trusting that what was meant to come through would come through for the highest benefit of all, irrespective of whether my ego liked it or not. This was somewhat disconcerting initially. I felt I had arrived somewhat naked and unprepared. However, I learned to lean into this discomfort and be in a state of surrender. This took the power, potency and depth of the sharing to a whole new level and it was a deeply relaxing experience for me as well. There was nothing to prove and so I was free from the hope that people would approve.

The Zen Peacemakers is a worldwide movement that has three tenets: Not Knowing, Bearing Witness, Taking Action. The first tenet, Not Knowing, invites us to hold lightly our fixed ideas about ourselves, others and the world. When we let go of what we have relied upon for a sense of self or stability, it can lead us to take shelter in a place where self-interest has not yet entered. This is essentially the same as being agendaless. It is a place of great wisdom and power. The next tenet, Bearing Witness, invites us to deeply connect with the joys and sorrows of others. This requires slowing down, listening deeply and relating beyond common assumptions and stereotypes. The third tenet, Taking Action, is the action that emerges from the previous two. It tends to be spontaneous and often surprising, yet it usually fits the situation perfectly.

You may have realized that we have almost never been without an agenda our entire lives. Even our morning walk comes with an agenda: keeping us fit or losing weight or completing ten thousand steps. Our whole life is one calculated program. When we are able to set down our agendas and simply show up, we open ourselves to guidance from our deeper intuitive selves and we are then able to welcome unexpected experiences and outcomes into our lives.

A Practice:

Ten seconds every hour, an hour or so every day, a day or so every week, a few days every month, maybe half a month to a month every year—make time to be 'agendaless'.

Every time you enter a space to meet someone, ask yourself: 'What is my agenda here? Can I hold it lightly? What is it like to be "agendaless"?'

Complete the following sentence with several examples:

'I am releasing the expectation that _____'
or it could be
'I am releasing the agenda to _____'

Section 2

Joyful Discoveries

8

My Quiet Rebellion

In a world of sorrow, I did not make,
a world I was given, I did not take,
let my joy be my quiet rebellion

in a world of hate and walls so high,
where fathers weep and children cry,
let my love be my quiet rebellion

in a world that clothes itself so well,
and wounds that fester, bleed and swell,
let my nakedness be my quiet rebellion

in a world of trade that measures worth,
that takes your soul to warm your hearth,
let empty hands be my quiet rebellion

in a world that tells me you're the other
you're not my friend, you're not my brother,
and we could never be the same,
our different faith, our different name,

can we not find our way to be?
our kinder, gentler way to see,
let our knowing be our quiet rebellion.

The Path of Dharma

Right here is a holy place; right here I will build my sanctuary.
                                        —Emila Heller

Let's start with a story. Zen Master Hakuin was praised and respected by his neighbours for his simplicity, virtue and the purity of his life. Near the place where he lived there was a food store. The owner had a beautiful, unmarried daughter.

One day she was discovered to be pregnant. Her parents flew into a rage. They wanted to know who the father was, but she would not give them the name. After repeated scolding and harassment, she finally confessed to them that Hakuin was the father of the unborn child. The parents were furious that the holy man they had respected all this time had turned out to be such a charlatan and imposter.

Along with a host of villagers, they went to Hakuin and roundly abused and scolded him. All he said in response to their angry accusations was: 'Is that so?'

When the child was born, they again went to Hakuin, and berating him in foul tongues, they left the newborn with him, saying that from here on, the child was his responsibility. Hakuin just said, 'Is that so?'

Without complaining he began taking good care of the child. By this time his reputation had been entirely sullied, and he was an object of mockery. Days ran into weeks, weeks into months and months into a full year.

Meanwhile, the young girl felt torn and tormented by her conscience because she held a terrible secret. One day she could not hold it in any longer and disclosed the name of the child's true father to her parents. A man who worked in a fish market had been her secret lover and she had falsely accused Hakuin to protect his identity.

The parents were aghast at this revelation and were filled with deep remorse, sorrow and regret. Along with dozens of villagers, they rushed to Hakuin, tearfully bowed and begged for his forgiveness as they narrated the entire story.

Hakuin listened to them and simply responded: 'Is that so?'

He blessed the infant and gracefully returned it to its mother with the same poise with which he had accepted it from her.

This story teaches us a powerful lesson in non-resistance. Whatever life presents to us, we have an opportunity to drop resistance and embrace the circumstances we often have no control over. The only thing we are responsible for is our state of being and our responses. Non-resistance is the foundation for genuine acceptance and wholesome actions. It also illustrates how true character is both forged and revealed in the process of responding to challenges. When we can't change the situations of our life, it may mean that they are here to change us.

This story is also a lesson in equanimity. True inner peace comes when we can respond to success and failure, praise and criticism with an equal mind. The Zen Master did not allow the unfair and unpleasant event to disturb his peace. This shows that our inner equilibrium need not be easily affected by the actions and opinions of others.

Hakuin simply followed his Dharma, or his intrinsic nature, without being influenced by events, circumstances, the opinions of others or even his own identity as a revered Zen Master.

We can live an entire lifetime consumed by our identities, our self-image and the expectations of others. Yet a fundamental question remains: How must one live? To know this, we need to examine the path of Dharma, or the wise way to live.

While there are many interpretations of Dharma, one of the most straightforward and powerful ways it can be framed is: Know yourself, discover your gifts and then use those gifts for the greatest good of all.

Knowing oneself means asking the fundamental question: 'Who am I?' Unlike other questions, the point here is not so much about finding a conclusive answer, it is about dissolving the questioner. This is a lifelong process which reliably brings us to a state of undiluted presence.

In my experience I have found that the more I question who I am, the more I find nothing concrete there. When I am not limited to a specific identity or quality, there is no opposition, and this reveals a natural connection with everything. This is freeing.

This awareness awakens all kinds of potential. Presence implies absence. The deeper the connection with presence, the fewer the assumptions of who we are. So now instead of being limited by our identities, there is space and freedom to express all aspects of ourselves—our gifts, our strengths and the blossoming of our natural genius.

Whether it is teaching or dancing or writing or leading, we all have our gifts. The more I allow my energy, my time and most importantly my attention to flow into those gifts, the better I get at them and the better I get at them, the more expansively I can let them flower.

How do we know what our gifts are? They are what is needed in the moment. If you show up with full presence; if you really show up, you are never unequal to the moment. If you show up beyond your identities, there is no mistake. There may be mental chatter such as 'I shouldn't be here, I'm not good enough or I'm an imposter,' but there is no mistake. You are exactly where you are meant to be. Therefore, the more you show up, the more you see; you are exactly what life is calling for in this moment. You are the medicine for this moment.

How do we define 'the greatest benefit of all'? To paraphrase theologian Fredrick Buechner,[9] do the work where your deep gladness and the world's deep hunger meet.

The way I define it for myself is that people who come in contact with me, or my teachings, receive an incorruptible seed of awakening. Which means that nothing can stop their intuitive wisdom from flowering from that point on. So, this is my intention and operating principle, whether or not other people are aware of it.

In India, there are three phrases that summarize the stages of spiritual maturity, which in turn impact the way we live our lives. They are *Bhogta Bhav, Drashta Bhav* and *Kevala Darshan.*

Bhogta Bhav (I am experiencing): One is completely identified with sense experiences (sights, sounds, smells, tastes, sensations and our thoughts about them). We see ourselves as the doer and the enjoyer, constantly seeking pleasant experiences and developing attachments. There is constant avoidance of unpleasant experiences, and anger and fear around them.

At this stage, the things that support us are association with the wise, gratitude, selfless service, reflection, meditation and not taking ourselves too seriously.

Drashta Bhav (I am witnessing experiences): This is the perspective of the observer, one who witnesses all sense experiences as they arise and pass away. What is needed is done with sincerity, attention, care and without stickiness. There is an ability to listen to the thoughts, opinions and voices in one's head without being compelled to follow them. This is the stage of witnessing consciousness. Things are happening and one watches the unfolding. At this stage, there tends to be more acceptance, flow and a sense of being—a channel of all actions rather than the doer.

In addition to the previous practices, at this stage, continuity of awareness, uncovering our shadows, exploring our assumptions, questioning our fondest beliefs, relating with mindfulness and steady, persistent self-inquiry are most supportive.

Kevala Darshan (Life experiencing itself): At this stage, even the sense of being a witness is questioned and transcended. Life experiences life. Everything seems to happen by itself, in a balanced and harmonious way. Also, in a sense nothing ever happens. There is unity of stillness and flow, like the dance of the ocean and its waves. Words like oneness and emptiness finally make sense.

Every experience supports, completes and fulfils itself. There is the full flowering of all latent talents and abilities as there are no inner resistances, inhibitions or doubts. This life is no longer personal, it is blessed and it is a blessing.

Another way to look at Dharma is through the lens of Persona, Presence and Essence.

Persona is the sense of *Karta Bhav* and *Bhogta Bhav*, the doer and the enjoyer, which is our personality, so we can imagine Persona is like a little bubble. Now imagine there is another bubble, an infinite bubble, without a visible beginning or end and the little bubble gently intersects with this infinite bubble and that point of touch, that contact, is Presence. Presence is the space from where you respond to your name, fully knowing that you are not that. You have a role, but you are not that role. Beyond both Persona and Presence, lies Essence. Essence is who you really are. Essence transcends and yet includes Persona and Presence. This is *Kevala Darshan*. Life is experiencing life.

The Japanese concept of *Ikigai* is another beautiful perspective on Dharma.

Ikigai comes from *iki* which means life and *gai* which comes from the word *kai* which translates to 'shell' in

Japanese. During the Heian period, shells were extremely valuable, so the association of value is still inherently seen in this word. *Gai* is the key to finding your purpose, or value in life. The basic ideology of *Ikigai* rests on four qualities—what you are good at, what the world needs, what you can be paid for and what you love. It is within the intersection of these four, that your *Ikigai* lives. *Ikigai* is the life purpose that gets you up every morning, keeps you going and gives meaning to your actions.

While there are different interpretations of Dharma across cultures and schools of thought, the defining principles remain constant—knowing oneself, understanding our own unique gifts and using them fruitfully for the greatest benefit of all.

Practices:

This is a powerful affirmation to help us tune in more deeply and joyfully into our purpose.

Magical seeds of infinite blessings are being planted in the deepest part of my consciousness. From here they take root and grow in abundant ways, and these blessings flower in all areas of my life. Without too much effort, I am able to access the field of blessings towards people, towards things and towards my own inner states, and merge with a field of blessings. This is inevitable. Nothing can stop this. No situation, no person, no amount of practice or non-practice will stop this. This is so inevitable, and I am so grateful.

Tathaastu! Tathaastu! Tathaastu! (And so it is, and so it is, and so it is!)

A Reflection on the Purpose of Life:

There are many ideas around the purpose of our life. Here are a few that have resonated with me. Reflect on these ideas and discuss them with your friends.

1. The purpose of life is to be ALIVE. So do whatever makes you come alive.
2. Do the work where your deepest gladness meets the world's greatest hunger.
3. The purpose of life is to find the purpose of life!
4. The purpose of life is to be present to life, now.
5. Our Dharma has three aspects: (1) Know oneself; (2) Discover one's gifts; (3) To use them for the highest benefit of others
   (i.e., To help them know themselves. Discover their gifts. Use them for the benefit of others.)
6. Do the work where all—(1) what you love (2) what you are good at and (3) what adds value to others—overlap.
7. Essentially our purpose is to be aware, and be loving.
8. We can find our life purpose by sitting undisturbed in a place and writing as many answers to the question 'What is my purpose?' until we arrive at an answer which gives us goosebumps or brings tears to our eyes. That is our life purpose.

9. Life is 'for-giving' love. Life is not 'for-getting' love.

10. God / Life does not choose our purpose, we choose our purpose. Decide it and start living, instead of waiting for perfect conclusions. For example, the purpose I have chosen is 'Spreading Happiness'.

11. Wisdom and Compassion: The intention to be fully enlightened for the benefit of all is the highest purpose.

12. The purpose of life is not about becoming, it is about being. From human to being, to being an integrated human being. From persona to essence, to an integrated presence.

13. Make a list of people, places, books, movies, music, etc., that inspire you. Ask yourself why they do. Distil the understanding to find your purpose.

14. What is the one per cent of your life that gives you ninety-nine per cent of your results? This is your genius, this is your purpose. Ask your friends and loved ones for feedback on this question.

15. What would you do with great joy if you had all the time and all the money in the world? This is your calling, your purpose.

16. Find one single word or quality that most inspires you. Make it your purpose.

17. Life has no purpose. We create one to satisfy our busy minds.

18. The meaning of life is to find your gift. The purpose of life is to give it away.

19. Imagine you have already achieved your full potential in all respects and are fully self-actualized. How do you describe who you are and your purpose?

20. Being where we are, and doing what we are doing with complete attention and love—this is the purpose of our life at any given moment.

9

Life as Mystery

Does the ash know, it was once a flame?
Does the puddle remember when it was rain?
Do the ones who pass know that once they lived,
and the newborn, from whence she came?

Is each thing whole, in the present complete?
The past, the future, do the edges meet?
So much forgotten, so much is lost,
An oak seed sleeps within deep frost,

but something hums from the realm of dark shadows,
and something binds our past to our morrows,
there are memories that live just beyond our grasp,
beyond our eyes, our minds, our clasp,

and the learned and the fool are equally blind,
equally lost to what's left behind,
some say they know but one journey's alone,
it cannot be learned, it cannot be shown,

the answers will come, for they're already there,
well sometimes it all seems a bit unfair,

to be given a mind that can question why,
that can dig so deep, that can soar so high,

but the answers are glimpses, a flicker, a wink,
a may be, a could be, a plausible think,
and seems like we'll know if we ever really do,
when there is no one around we could tell it to!

Gamify the Spiritual Process

When we spell it out, we cast a spell.

I want to begin with an example that really opened my mind in a way I wasn't expecting. I was in high school and living in Gurgaon at that time. I would go to New Delhi to meet some teachers and friends. One day on the bus, I saw a lady reading a book that seemed quite interesting. So, I asked her, 'Do you mind if I ask what book you're reading?' She said, 'Sure,' and showed me the book. It was *Notes to Myself*,[10] a famous book by Hugh Prather. We began talking and she said something that I have never forgotten. She said, 'I've learnt something. Whenever I have a question, I formulate the question with a lot of clarity. Then I walk to my bookshelf and I pull out any book. I open any page and I read any line and I find the answer.' I was left wondering how that was even possible!

I felt like I had to try this. I went home that evening and I formulated a question. I went to the bookshelf and just let my hand find a book. I opened a random page and began reading a random line. As I contemplated that line, it actually made sense. It just blew my mind. So, I tried it again. Each time, with a little bit of focus, I found that it worked. It completely shifted the way I looked at life and the universe. I no longer perceived the universe only as a physical place populated with things. I began to see it as a highly reflective field of intelligence that flawlessly mirrors every thought, feeling and action.

This is one of the first memories I have of a playful and experimental way to activate the power of intention. Since then, I have experienced the power of trusting this deeper intelligence of life in countless ways.

Once, I came up with an intention game and wanted to test it with my friends. We were going on a long drive. I invited them to say something that they would like to see. For instance, to see a man in a yellow turban. Then we would all spend about a minute visualizing what was said and looking out for it. So, we tried it and sure enough, after a while, we actually began seeing the things we had visualized.

My friends thought that maybe this was a coincidence and we should do it again. I thought of a group of people who were holding hands and walking together. Shortly after, we saw some people holding hands. It was amazing. One person in our group was really sceptical and felt we were asking for simple things. So, he came up with something unlikely. He said, 'I want to see a dinosaur. And if that happens, I'll really believe that there's something to this.'

So, we all visualized that for about a minute. After a while we stopped to fill fuel in the car. Right there at the gas station was a big dinosaur statue. We were all so delighted!

It's strange how these intention games can resolve problems as well. Once, I was teaching at a session in Bangalore. I told the group to arrive the next day at five minutes to nine so that we start the session sharp at nine. An elderly gentleman came up to me and said, 'Nithya, I can only come at eleven. I live very far away and I have to change four buses to come here. There's no way I can come before eleven.' So, I said, 'Well, you've learnt the power of intention. So, go back and try it. See what happens.' He was quite sceptical.

The next morning, he came exactly on time and shared his experience before the session began. He said, 'I woke up in the morning and vividly visualized getting here on time. I went to the bus stop and the first bus was already there waiting for me. I boarded it. The same thing happened for the other three buses as well. I barely had to wait a few minutes between each bus! This is the first time this has happened to me in my forty-year history of travelling in Bangalore by bus. I am amazed and don't know how to explain this!'

He didn't have to explain. Everything in life need not be explained. Just play with it. We don't have to get analytical about everything. Just be playful about these things.

I remember having lunch with the founder of one of the largest software companies in India. He said, 'Nithya, I really agree with your teaching about the power of intention and I'd like to share my story. When I got married, my wife and I made a list of intentions and dreams. We wanted to have homes in different countries. We wanted a foundation that could serve many people. At that time, the things we wrote seemed so far-fetched since we were just starting out and had limited means. A few months back, my wife was clearing out a cupboard and she found an old piece of paper—it was our list of intentions. She came to me and said that we have to make a new list. All of this has happened.'

I was once at a retreat in the Netherlands. During a morning walk, a friend shared something fascinating with me. He introduced me to a game which he claimed could change one's life forever. In this game, once every minute you are to tell yourself something awesome about yourself, and keep doing this for two hours!

I loved this idea and so on our walk itself, we began playing this awesomeness game. We took turns to share with each other what we found awesome about ourselves. After a while, I changed the game a little and began to tell him what was awesome about him. Similarly, he began to tell me what was awesome about me. Later, we started saying what was awesome about us, about the place we were at, about life, and we got so carried away that we literally lost our way! It took us two hours to get back and even on the way back, we kept playing. That experience is still etched in my memory so clearly. How often do we spend two continuous hours focusing on nothing but what's awesome?

Another interesting game to play draws upon the realization that time is not an objective thing. I have sometimes offered extended practice sessions for twelve hours or more where people who have never meditated before have said they were amazed at how quickly time seemed to pass. This is because time is malleable; our experience of it can expand or contract, depending on our state of mind and the focus of our attention.

When I have a long flight for instance, I inwardly say, 'Time will contract.' What would otherwise be an eighteen- or twenty-two-hour journey feels like a two- or three-hour journey. This is my lived experience. On the other hand, when I'm enjoying something, such as meeting friends after a long time, but we are together for just a few hours, I inwardly say, 'Time will expand.' Those two to three hours somehow feel like a whole day.

This happens in other scenarios as well. There were occasions when I was requested to condense my hour-long talk to forty minutes since the previous speaker had overshot their time. But you know what? Time will expand. Everything I want to do in that hour, I will do in merely forty minutes, and it's possible that I will do it better than I would have in an hour.

I want to share something of great significance. Consider not thinking of your brain as a hard-disk drive where memories, experiences and learnings are stored. I recommend you see your brain as a modem or Wi-Fi router. In other words, you are not limited to local storage and you have broadband access to infinite intelligence. Much like how a router connects to the internet, you too can connect to the 'inner-net', to the universal intelligence. This shift in perception expands your sense of resourcefulness.

We are not limited to our life experiences. We have access to all wisdom, all intelligence and all knowledge across space and time. As unbelievable as this may sound, consider the possibility that we are not limited to the past, or even the future. 'What if we have intuitive access right now, to the things we are going to learn in the future?' This is because one is tapping into a universal mind, a universal consciousness. These are not things to be believed, they are to be experimented with in the crucible of our own life.

A friend of mine had been looking for a house in Singapore for a while, and since his lease was expiring soon, he was rather stressed. We spoke and I asked him to play with the perception that everything has consciousness. So, this means that places and spaces also have consciousness. Therefore, just as he had been looking for a place, many places were also looking for someone like him. Those places would also like to have a loving, wholesome family like his. This way of looking at things helped ease his anxiety and he began to trust that something would work out soon. That what he was seeking was equally seeking him. Sure enough, he found a place very quickly and was thrilled that it seemed to have worked.

The idea is to approach all these things with a light and playful spirit. More often than not, it will work out well. What if it doesn't work out as expected? Then trust that something even better is coming. This is important. Don't hold intentions tightly and seriously. Have a sense that you are already fulfilled, already complete. A profound verse from the Isha Upanishad elaborates on this idea:

Om poornam adaha poornam idam poornaath poornam udachyate, poornasya poornam aadhaaya poornam evaavasishyathe, Om Shantihi Shantihi Shantihi.

This is complete, that is complete. From the complete, comes the complete. When completeness is removed from completeness, what is left is also complete. May there be peace, peace, peace.

Practices:

Play with the power of intention. Focus on what you want to see for about a minute and feel the joy like it is already so. Then let go and trust that you will be guided.

Try the Awesomeness game with a partner. For ten seconds every minute, each of you share something awesome about yourselves. You can practise this as long as you can keep going but a reasonable start would be for ten or fifteen minutes. Be aware of what rises within you during and at the end of this practice.

10

Trust

To dive deep with those
Who merely like to sail over the waters in a pretty boat,
to lose yourself in the patterns of seashells
amongst those,
who only admire the pearls strung upon your neck,
and ask you what they cost,
to live, this way, with half a breath,
is to live, but barely.

Like migratory birds that fly great distances,
because something in them knows they must,
you too will travel,
leaving the safety of the known,
alone perhaps but with fierce resolve,
into the deepest recesses of your being

for you have come from afar,
across unfathomable distances,
from your home in the stars that have
long disappeared into nothingness,
and you have birthed yourself across
lifetimes unknown,
into your now,
another ocean beckons.

The Four Levels of Consciousness

When we change the way we look at things, the things we
look at change

One of my favourite stories is of an old man, renowned for instantly solving people's problems. From all over the world, the distressed would come to him and he would say, 'Don't tell me the problem. Take this handkerchief and write your problems on it.' So, they would, in great detail, 'I lost my business' or 'I lost my home', and return the handkerchief to him with hopeful hearts.

The old man would then point to a big tree behind him and people would see that there were thousands of handkerchiefs tied all over it. He would ask them to tie theirs as well. Upon their return, he would say, 'I have a gift. I can exchange problems. Go find a problem that is less intense than yours and I can exchange it with the one you have.' People would go and open one handkerchief after another and find problems such as 'I lost my child' or 'I lost my leg' or 'I have an incurable disease.' Instantly people would balk and think, 'I don't want those problems!' They would then realize that their problem was just right for them.

We often think our issues are the worst of all but when we start to pay close attention to other people's lives, even the ones that appear picture-perfect, we might realize that we are actually not that badly off and perhaps we might even find ourselves thankful for our own problems. Compared to someone, your problems are acute, yet compared to someone else your problems are very cute. A shift in our way of thinking is all it takes to gain a wider perspective. A powerful principle is that when we change our way of looking at things, the things we look at change.

Within every problem is a beautiful possibility. Within every possibility is pure joy. Within the joy is the present moment. Within the present moment is our true nature. What we focus on expands.

A Sufi master once asked her student to bring her a glass of water and some salt. He did. She asked him to put a heaped spoonful of salt in the glass of water. The puzzled student did as he was told. 'Now drink the water,' she instructed. The student attempted to but made a face. 'It's too salty!' he complained. So, she smiled and asked him to bring a bucketful of water. Again, she asked him to put a heaped spoonful of salt in it and mix it in until it dissolved. 'Now taste the water,' she repeated. He tried and said, 'This time I can barely taste the salt.' Next, the master led the student to a large freshwater lake. She asked him to put a heaped spoonful of salt into the lake and mix it up. She asked the student to taste the water. He did and said, 'I can't taste any salt at all!'

The master questioned him: 'What remained constant?' The student replied: 'The quantity of salt.' She asked: 'What changed?' The student said: 'The amount of water.' The master then explained that the spoonful of salt represents the problems in our life and the water represents what we are thankful for. We often cannot control the amount of salt in our lives, but we can increase the amount of water.

The more expansively we can see the possibilities, the less intense our problems will appear. When the focus remains solely on the problem, we are operating from the lowest level of consciousness. The attention remains on what should not be: what our spouse should not be doing, what our children should not be doing, our pet should not be doing, even our neighbour's pet should not be doing. In this state, for us to be happy, or fulfilled, we believe that everything around us needs to change first. It is hard for us to consider the possibility that something might have to change in us. This stage of being is also known as **unconscious non-intention.**

Unconscious means not being attentive to our present experience. It means being completely enmeshed in the story of the past and the future. The truth is that what we *think* happened is merely one perspective. There are infinite perspectives to understand the past and infinite possibilities for the future. When there is little acceptance, gratitude or love for the past, and we project from this state of being into the future, we are bound to remain in a perpetual cycle of fear and trepidation. Hence, if we want to clean up our future, it becomes necessary to clean up our past.

How do we do this? We do this by cleaning up our thoughts about the past, and bringing the blessings which came out of our experiences into focus. Events of the past can be viewed from many perspectives. If we stay fixated on a single story, then we limit ourselves and project these limitations into the future. This state of unconscious non-intention simply means not knowing what we want, while our entire focus remains on what we don't want.

The next level of consciousness is 'Happiness for a relative reason' which is tied to the myth of 'when' and the myth of 'more'. The myth of when is this: I will be happy *when* something happens or *when* I can finally own something I desire such as a bike, a car or a house. It is based on an acquisitive mindset and happiness is always one object of desire away, until an entire life is spent chasing the next thing to own, experience or feel.

In India, children are often told, first study well at school, get into a good college and *then* you will be happy. When you go to college and study hard, you will get a good job and *then* you will be happy. When you work hard and get promoted, *then* you will be happy. Once you are married, *then* you will be happy. Have children, and *then* you will be happy. When you have your own home, *then* you will be happy. Get a bigger home, buy two cars, and *then* you will be happy. When your kids grow up and settle down, *then* you will be happy. It is always the next thing. So finally, when you do have little grandchildren and you're sitting with them at home and watching television, a Guru will come on one of the religious channels and say, 'Don't worry, be well behaved in this life and *then* in your next life you will be happy!'

The myth of 'more' is blindly following what other people are doing. If someone buys a big house, we want that house. If they get a new car, we want the car. If they send their children to a particular school, now we want our children in that school too. This is a universal sentiment because many of us have a deep-seated need to fit in, to conform, to be validated. This is happiness for a 'relative' reason because it is an 'outside-in' kind of happiness. Even if you get it—the house, the car, the school—the satisfaction is neither deep nor lasting. This state of consciousness is higher than the first one because it generates energy. You are more affirmative—'Yes I can' and 'Yes I will'—and so in one sense it has value, but in another sense, it is lacking, because it is again focused on outer circumstances for inner happiness. The truth is that when we are always focused on the outside, we will not be at peace, since there will always be a fear of losing it. This is the state of **Unconscious Intention.**

The way to rise to the third level of consciousness is to ask ourselves three powerful questions:

1. What do I want?
2. How would it feel to have it?
3. Can I feel that right now?

These three questions convert expectations into intentions. They help us shift from a state of longing to fulfilment. We come into vibrational alignment with what we want. This awakens deeper creative and intuitive guidance within us that lead us towards what we seek.

One clarifying exercise is to ask why we want anything. This is to reveal the primary need underlying our wants.

One process is to ask 'Why' seven or more times until we arrive at something irreducible. Here is an example . . .

An exchange could something like this:

What do you really want?
To have more uninterrupted time to write and express myself creatively.

Why do you want to express yourself?
It helps me understand myself better.

Why do you want to understand yourself better?
I want to understand myself better because I feel there are unresolved things within me that I want to examine.

Why do you want to resolve these things?
I feel like they block or come in the way of me being my most natural self.

Why do you want to be your most natural self?
I would feel untangled within and expressive in my writings.

Why do you want to feel untangled and expressive?
I would then be able to write more, share my work with more people and gain confidence in myself.

Why do you want to write more and share your work?
It would make me happy and give me the freedom to do what I consider my life's work.

So, the primary need here is happiness and freedom. How do we reach this state of being? Can we get there from a place of lack and disconnection? We can do things *for* happiness or we can do things *from* happiness. How much more harmonious life would be if we were to *begin* from those inner states we seek. It is important to realize that all states of being are available and accessible to us at all times, independent of extraneous factors and circumstances. This is the state of **Conscious Intention**.

Let me introduce a radical idea. In the present moment there are never any problems. Life just is the way it is. Problems come from judgement, comparison and resistance. By itself an experience is pleasant or unpleasant or neutral and it is what it is. When we get present, an intuitive recognition arises that this too shall pass and the next step naturally reveals itself. When there is something to be done, we give it everything we have got. When there is nothing to be done, we pause and trust and do nothing. *When strong, serve. When weak, surrender.*

There is a simple way to come to the present moment. See what you're seeing, hear what you're hearing, feel what you're feeling and ask yourself this simple question—'Am I okay in this precise moment?' Most people who are asked this question, respond saying, 'Yes, in this precise moment I am okay!' If you are okay in this precise moment, every decision you ever made in your life was the right decision. It got you to this point of okay. The story ends well! Any other decision would have got you somewhere else. The more present you are, the more you lose your fear of decision-making. You realize you can take any path and it will be okay. This is the fourth level of consciousness—**Conscious Non-intention.**

So, the four levels of consciousness we talked about are:

Unconscious Non-Intention: Focusing on what you don't want—the problem. This is the stage of victimhood.

The second, **Unconscious Intention**: Focusing on what you do want, which forms the realm of possibilities, ambitions, acquisitions.

The third is **Conscious Intention**: This is the stage of clarity of purpose, and entails living and working from the root desire without waiting for external events and circumstances to align.

The fourth is **Conscious Non-Intention**: It is the state of simply being, simply being present, simply being awake.

Practices:

Every day as you awaken, say: 'May I be a channel of blessings for someone today. May I be the clearest possible channel of the highest possible blessings for someone today.' And so it is!

Begin your day with gratitude. A simple practice is 'The Lotus of Gratitude'. Imagine each of your hands is a lotus flower and open each of your fingers like they are petals of the lotus flower as you count ten things you are grateful for. In the end, you bring both the opened lotus flowers close to your heart and imagine that there are two lotus flowers close to your heart. Simply say: Thank you!

11

Little Things

I like the idea of a forbidding, impenetrable castle
with a secret little door open
only for strays and wastrels.
I like the idea of strangers swapping headphones
to listen to each other's songs.
I like the silver-haired lady at the check-in counter
with polka dot fingernails and a smile
that reaches the corners of her eyes.
I like smooth stones that can skip three times over water
And the men who know how to make them.
I like to see my mother dance,
when her favourite song comes on.
I like people who make terrible excuses
just so they can stay home and read.
I like to watch dogs dream
and then jump up at the slightest sound.
I like being alone in noisy, bustling places
and sharing quiet places with my favourite people.
I like to look out of windows.
I like making lists of the things I like.

Rampage of Appreciation

What we appreciate, appreciates

An intention I have for this work is that those who come in contact with these teachings are among the top five per cent most grateful people in the world, and preferably among the 0.1 per cent. This implies drastically reducing how much we complain and dramatically increasing moments of appreciation and connection for and with everything around us.

An interesting way to think about appreciation is with the analogy of a car. The accelerator pedal represents saying 'yes'. It stands for all that we love, admire, appreciate and wish to experience more of in our life. The brake pedal represents saying 'but,' which stands for all the obstacles, limitations, unworthiness and the voice of the inner critic. Most of us are conditioned to drive through life with an expansive 'yes,' followed by the immediate negation of 'but'. Often when it comes to other people, our approach is: 'I'll appreciate you, but I'll also tell you how you need to get better.' We are conditioned to appreciate each other but also directly or subtly, pull that person down in the fear of fanning their ego.

It almost seems easier to go on a rampage of criticism. Many of us have experienced this—people have been disappointed or enraged by the perceived faults and weaknesses they see in us, and then started offering unsolicited advice on what we should be changing or how we can improve. This could be from a family member, a friend, a teacher, a colleague at work or even a person who barely knows us. To have experienced a rampage of appreciation is rather rare. This implies someone has pressed the accelerator pedal and focused only on the big yes by sharing all the things that they unequivocally love and appreciate about another.

There are three facets of appreciation: the way we have been in the past, the way we are now and of course, the greater potential that exists within us. Apart from these, there is another powerful way to appreciate someone— by telling them how they impact us. For example, 'When I'm with you, I just lose track of time' or 'When I'm with you, I always learn something new' or 'When I'm with you, it always uplifts me.' It is so wonderful to receive this appreciation without the pressing of the brake pedal.

There is a story of a tribe in Africa, which has an unusual tradition. Whenever someone in the tribe behaves in a way that is hurtful or violates the tribe's norms—such as taking something that is not theirs, or being physically or verbally abusive—he or she is considered to be severely ill. The notion is that someone who is in a state of inner and outer wellbeing cannot intentionally do something to hurt others in the tribe.

The entire village stops everything that they're doing and gathers around this person who is seated alone and unfettered in the centre of a circle. One by one, every man, woman and child in the tribe comes up to the person and recounts in as much detail as possible every memory of this person doing something kind, selfless or loving. This ceremony can sometimes take days and the tribe members are not allowed to do any other work during this time. They have to sit there and follow through with this ceremony because they want this person to heal. At the end of the ceremony, there's a joyful celebration and this person is lovingly welcomed back into the tribe.

This approach is so refreshingly different from the usual punitive approach that most societies follow. Seldom do we consider the underlying individual and systemic causes for harmful actions in the first place. The African tribe says we've got it backwards. If a person is behaving in this way, it means something in all of us needs healing. By the power of love, appreciation and forgiveness, collective healing is possible.

While this tribe sets a high benchmark, even a little appreciation can take us a long way on the path of healing. A few kind words are enough to make someone's day. One of my teachers, Ajahn Brahm, said that when you are telling someone that you appreciate them, speak for at least fifteen seconds. Why is that? He said that it takes at least fifteen seconds for people to register and realize that you mean it. This is because often we say things like 'good job', 'well done' or 'very nice' that sound like empty platitudes. If you really want to appreciate someone, you have to elaborate on how they have impacted you. Look into their eyes, smile and make an effort to connect. Usually when someone criticizes us, we realize it within half a second and all our emotional defences come up. On the other hand, when someone appreciates us, we can find it hard to believe and wonder if they really mean it. Given how most of us are unaccustomed to receiving wholehearted appreciation, it is important to convey the sincerity of our words.

Let me share an example of how one company used the power of appreciation to create a motivated workforce. I was teaching at a pharmaceutical company called Sundyota Numandis in Ahmedabad. I noticed that they have a unique way to welcome new employees. At the end of the induction process, a letter goes to their parents saying that their child has successfully finished their training and is now a part of the company. The letter says that the company is happy to have him or her on board. What the letter says next is what sets this company apart. It reads, 'This was made possible because of all the years that you put in giving them good values and a good education, so we are really indebted to you.' Parents who received this letter were often moved to tears. Some of them would even tease their children saying that the company had appreciated them more than they ever had.

So, what next? Of course, everyone is uplifted. The employee is happy and motivated to work with such a good company. The parents have a sense of goodwill towards the organization. A happier workforce leads to a more productive workplace and a congenial atmosphere for all. With one act of appreciation, the company has achieved so much.

I will share another remarkable story of appreciation. A friend of mine, Hema Hattangady used to run Conzerv, an energy management company in Bengaluru. She wanted to make a corporate film, which would explain the company ethos and values. Instead of hiring a media agency to do this, she decided to get the employees of the company to make the film themselves. Why? She felt that her employees would have a deeper understanding of the context and culture compared to an external agency. The challenge was that the employees didn't have any professional videography or editing skills. So, she hired experts who could teach them these skills.

To make it more interesting, she involved employees from various departments and received a huge response. Many employees wanted to be a part of this filmmaking project so she turned it into a contest where the best film would win a prize of one lakh rupees. She set up five teams, which included members from various departments and across different levels. Over the next few months, each member of the five teams learned a new skill related to this project. They also got to know each other better. They asked each other important questions: What are the values of our company? What is the mission of our company? What is the unique DNA of our company?

Once all the films were ready, a gala event was hosted. The employees' families were invited and all the films were showcased. Hema felt that all the films were well made. So, on the spot she announced that all the five teams were the winners and each would receive one lakh rupees. Can you believe the energy in the room when she announced this? Everyone attending burst into applause and each one

of them felt so proud to be part of this organization. As a
leader, Hema achieved something remarkable. She found
a way to get many people in the organization to reflect
deeply about what the company meant to them and to
work together as teams to achieve a common goal. The
whole exercise ended in a rampage of appreciation which
uplifted the entire community.

My friends and I practise a more intense version of this
and we call it a rampage of appreciation. We choose one
person in the group and take no less than fifteen minutes
to shower the person with *truthful* appreciation of what we
love about them and the deeper potentials we see in them.
With this the entire energy of the body shifts. This happens
because we don't realize how each one of us, at some level,
is constantly judging ourselves. We're criticizing ourselves;
we're being hard on ourselves. Outwardly, we may look
very put together, but inwardly we're all fighting our own
private battles.

When we hear unqualified appreciation, it directly
undermines the inner critic. Receiving so much appreciation
and acknowledgement can feel somewhat disorienting and
unbelievable at first, but soon our inner critic surrenders
and we feel light, clear and strong.

A Practice:

There are five elements to this practice of appreciation.

First, look around your room and focus on an object
that is adding value to your life. Look at it from your heart

and not just with your eyes. See what it feels to be that object and remain unnoticed for how it is contributing to your life, while it is giving its 100 per cent. Next, get back to being you and for fifteen seconds, go on a rampage of appreciation for this object, connecting with it from your heart to its heart. And as you're doing it, notice the emotion rising within each cell of your body, connecting with the object so deeply. Take a deep breath and every day, wherever you are and whenever you remember this exercise, look at any object in front of you and connect with it in the same way.

The second step is to think about a person who has impacted your life. This could be anyone, close to you or far away, living or someone who has passed. All you have to do is truly connect with that person.

The third step is to look at someone in your family whom you have neglected and taken for granted or who you have not appreciated ever. Take time to think of him or her and truly connect with the person. Thank the person for their silent, generous and forgiving nature that kept giving even though you didn't acknowledge their contribution to your life.

The fourth one is to look at an object in nature. For example, it could be the trees around you, it could be the sunlight that brings the plants in your garden to life or anything else in nature. Look at the object and inhale deeply, thinking of the myriad ways in which it brings joy to your life every day. Focus on the feeling of joy and find yourself becoming one with nature.

The fifth one is to appreciate something in yourself and connect with that aspect of you that you've not paid much attention to. It could be something physical or an intangible quality such as a certain skill or ability like reading that you take for granted. Promise to cherish this quality if only to remind yourself that it is this that makes you who you are.

Appreciate these five gifts that are all around you and within you as often as you can.

12

Generous

Breath, sight, touch,
limbs that comply,
textures of skin, songbirds,
an open sky, the music of the waves,
the hush before the rain,
blueberries,
the scent of pine carried by the mountain air,
fingertips, gooseflesh,
the song that can hold a human heart,
warm cinnamon toast,
sheltered alleyways with little bookstores,
moon-kissed nights,
puppy eyes and kittens who won't beg for a treat,
strawberry fields and stained mouths,
silver anklets,
grandfather clocks and red oxide floors,
the first snow,
smooth pebbles, cool within warm palms,
a cup of tea, in bed,
your voice.
Life is generous, is it not?
In little, forgivable ways.

Intensity of Gratitude

Wear gratitude like a cloak and it will feed every corner of your life.

—*Rumi*

In a Native American tribe during the day, the men would go gathering food while the women got busy with their own duties. All the children were left with an elderly grandfather who knew that the best way to keep children engaged was to tell them stories. Each day the children asked the grandfather to tell them a new story. One day, the grandfather said, 'In everyone's life there are two wolves. One represents all the things that pull you down such as jealousy, judgement, anger, sadness and resentment. The other wolf represents all things which lift you up such as kindness, gratitude, compassion and love. These two wolves have a tremendous fight.' At this, the grandfather was quiet. All the kids were eagerly waiting for the grandfather to finish the story, but he remained silent. Finally, one child could not contain herself and asked, 'So grandpa, which of them is going to win?' The grandfather looked directly at her and said, 'The one that you feed.'

Every moment we are feeding one of the two wolves. Every moment we are practising something. At the very least our attention is either dispersed or focused. We are practising contentment or discontentment, connection or disconnection, clarity or confusion. We are either cultivating something skilful, or we are getting carried away by past unconscious conditioning. At every moment, what we practise grows stronger.

It would greatly benefit us to develop the muscle of gratitude. One way we can practise gratitude is during our meals. It takes a lot for our food to come to us. Chances are someone planted the crops, they were then harvested, transported, cooked and served. If we look deeply, we will find that it takes the whole universe to grow a single grain of rice. I remember when I was a monk, someone gave me coconut water. I finished it in about fifteen seconds. The person who offered it smiled at me and said, 'Do you know it took ten months to grow?' I had to sheepishly accept that it would be appropriate for me to take a few moments to appreciate and acknowledge the journey of my food before devouring it.

There is a lovely teaching: No one owes me anything. This is a useful principle to keep in mind. If we think people owe us anything, we will have a sense of entitlement. When we have a sense of entitlement, it's only a matter of time before we are disappointed because other people are not here to fulfil our expectations.

The difference then, is in the way we think about things. It's not what is happening, it's our story about what is happening. We are all playing this game all the time in the way we look at things. A good practice is to be mindful of your perceptions throughout the day and no matter what happens, say 'How wonderful'. Something so simple can make a big difference. In the beginning, you may feel like it is artificial, or seems inauthentic but the truth is that every thought we believe is artificial. Every thought, every perception tells an incomplete story. There is no thought that is the ultimate, all-encompassing reality. We are simply conditioned to think a certain way.

No matter what happens, say 'How wonderful'. Once, when I was in Delhi there was a dust storm, and all the flights were delayed. Since everybody's flight was delayed, the whole airport was packed with people. Everyone was upset. The weather was the way it was, so nothing could be done. I just said, 'How wonderful.'

Sure enough, in that busy airport, I met three different people I knew. We were all so happy to meet each other and had a good time catching up. The third person was actually going through a very difficult time in his life, and he was really disturbed. Because our flight was so delayed, I got to spend two hours with this person. As we finally said goodbye, he said, 'Nithya, the storm is here, so you could be with me.' So, from one perspective a situation can be terrible, but from another, it could be exactly what someone needed. The more you practise welcoming everything and see how that shifts your entire outlook, the more you have the sense that 'Everything is happening as it should,' and you stop complaining. You trust that there is an underlying order animating all things and you align yourself with it.

I once read about a man who was going from Pune to Mumbai, and the bus stopped to allow passengers to take a break. He went to the bathroom, came back and the bus was leaving without him. He tried to stop the bus but couldn't. He was so upset and angry as his bag was on the bus and he was left behind. Few hours later that bus was in an accident and the majority of people died or were severely injured. This man, of course, survived. He said when he heard about the accident, in an instant, all that anger turned into infinite gratitude. We can never know the larger picture; we don't know how everything fits together. So, we just stay with the thumb rule that whatever is happening is happening for the best. We may not understand or like it, we just decide that it is the best thing that is happening.

There are powerful examples of people having this kind of trust and gratitude under very trying circumstances. In 1975, Arthur Ashe became the first African American to win the Gentlemen's Singles at Wimbledon. Some years later, he needed a blood transfusion and through the transfusion he got the HIV infection. In those days, the checks were not as stringent as they are today. He was asked once why he had to suffer such a terrible fate when he was a good man who never harmed anyone. He replied, 'All over the world some million teenagers aspire to become tennis players. Out of these million, may be a hundred thousand reach to some sort of proficiency. Of them, only a few thousand play in some circuit and only a hundred or so play the grand slam. Finally, only two reach the final of Wimbledon. When I was standing with the trophy of Wimbledon in my hand, I never questioned God "Why Me?" And now what right do I have to ask God "Why Me?"' [11]

Another beautiful example is that of Alice Herz-Sommer, who survived the Holocaust. She was put in the concentration camp and they realized that she was a good piano player, so they let her play piano. She played the piano with such heart and soul that even the guards would come and listen and say that when she played the piano, they forgot all their troubles. She was so cheerful and positive that even as a Jew in the concentration camp, she kept her faith. She went on to live to a hundred and twelve.

In a documentary about her life, *The Lady in Number 6* [12] Alice says that she was the only one in her building who smiled. Everyone was always upset and stressed out. She lived in London at the time. It was remarkable to see that someone who had lived through the Holocaust could be that happy and free. She was not cursing; she was not bitter. Once, a German journalist and his crew went to interview her and he was a little afraid of whether she would judge him harshly. They were surprised to find her open-hearted and loving. He asked if she was angry with them. She simply replied that it was not him and what happened was a long time ago. She did not hold a grudge against all Germans.

However, the Holocaust was not the only difficult thing to have happened to her. Her son died at the age of sixty-four. He was a world-class cello player. He came home one day complaining of a stomach-ache and they took him to the doctor to find his appendix had ruptured. By the next day, he had passed. In the documentary, when she remembered her son's passing, she grew quiet for a moment but very quickly she gathered herself and just said that she was grateful that he did not have to suffer for long and that he died rather quickly. Even in that loss, she found something to be grateful for.

If someone like Alice Herz-Sommer, whose family members had been systematically taken away and executed, whose son died, who had been through the savagery and inhumanity of a concentration camp could be grateful, cheerful and happy, then perhaps we too can find it in us to be more resilient through the ups and downs of life.

I find that like any other practice that is repeated often enough, an attitude of gratitude can become a way of life. Through our day there are infinite things we can be grateful for, if we wish to see them and acknowledge them. Let us always be aware of which wolf we are feeding, for that is the wolf that will win.

Practices:

Write down 108 things you are grateful for and add five more every day. Continue this list as long as you wish to.

Before you go to bed, challenge yourself to think of three to five things that went well in the day and write them down on a piece of paper or on your phone. As you focus on these, you will see a shift, you will start to feel like it was a good day. Another thing you can add to this is to ask yourself, 'How would I like to wake up tomorrow morning?' For example: 'I would like to wake up feeling energized, enthusiastic, with a new solution to this challenge I am facing.' This is a powerful way of taking the power of suggestion into your deeper mind.

13

Be Here Now

Strength is not an abstraction.
It calls for presence.
For waking up each day, each moment to what is.
A gathering, of the available,
to play with a dealt hand,
a letting go of what isn't.
Face the mirror, do the work.
Shoes, keys, food.
The now. Only the now.
Owed nothing, to stay kind.
Owed nothing, to show up.
And allow, for grief, for rage,
allow for the keening, the breaking apart, the buckled
knees, the hands that cover a flushed, wet, face.
Allow for lost, for not knowing, for help.
Not to be strong or be anything that is not the truth.
Only to allow, in time, a return to self,
to centre.
And as true as the falling of the leaves, the first flush
of spring,
the rise and the ebb of the tides,
as true as all that is born and dies,
to know,
all will pass, all is love.

Preparation and Practice

Meeting life without resistance

A group of people from the United Kingdom came to practise at Wat Nong Pa Pong, Ajahn Chah's monastery in Thailand. After a few weeks, it was time for them to depart and they came to him to pay respects and bid farewell. While expressing their gratitude for their time at the monastery, the leader of the group said, 'We have had a fruitful two months. We have grown so much in our practice. However, we have a concern which we are hoping you will resolve. Soon we will be back to our busy lives at home. We are worried that we might lose the precious rhythm that we established in our practice here. How do we keep this momentum going once we get back to our busy lives with so many responsibilities, duties and distractions? Is it even possible?'

Ajahn Chah smiled and said, 'When you think of practice, you think of sitting meditation, walking meditation, you think of chanting and reading scriptures, but that is not practice. That is preparation. Practice happens when unwanted things happen and wanted things don't happen in the day. When someone treats you the way you don't want to be treated or when something you expected is not given to you, that's the moment when the real practice happens. That's the moment when your underlying tendencies get activated. We can appear very unruffled when things happen our way, but what happens when the unwanted things happen?'

Ajahn Chah went on to say, 'Don't measure your practice by how many hours a day you are meditating or how consistent you are. We can do many things mechanically, some of us are temperamentally more suited to meditation and because of our personalities, we might be able to meditate regularly. The important thing to remember is that this is preparation. Our daily life is our real practice.'

What then is the measure of progress in our practice? It is simply in how balanced our minds are through the ups and downs of life. There will be praise, there will be blame, there will be comfort, there will be discomfort. There will be gain, there will be loss. Each one of us goes through happiness and sorrow in a lifetime. There is a beautiful teaching by the Buddha on the vicissitudes of life. In the 'Mangala Sutta', he describes the thirty-eight highest blessings. He says the highest blessing amongst all is: 'In the ups and downs of life keep a balanced mind.'

Phuṭṭhassa loka-dhammehi, cittaṃ yassa na kampati
Asokaṃ virajaṃ khemaṃ, etam mangalam uttamaṃ.

One who does not waver, when in contact with the vicissitudes of the world,
And remains sorrowless, stainless and secure; this is the highest blessing.

Our experiences change throughout the day and even moment to moment. As we realize the changing nature of phenomena, we do not tremble, shake or get agitated. We remain stainless, sorrowless, pure and secure. In the Bhagavad Gita, this state of being is called *Sthitaprajna*. This is the one whose wisdom does not shake or waver in the oscillations of life.

Every moment is ripe for awakening. Not just our so-called spiritually charged ones. Through our daily lives, in the moment when our underlying tendencies towards greed, aversion and confusion get activated, and we wake up to how none of this is really who we are, they are simply visitors, this is where a micro liberation occurs. In that moment, we can access the power of PAUSE, between stimulus and response, that's where wisdom lives. The idea is to access the pause with greater awareness. In the beginning we may catch ourselves after the event, but with presence we begin to catch ourselves before and during the event. We ask ourselves these questions: What just happened? What was just said? What thought was believed? Was it skilful, was it wholesome, was it beneficial? What might need to be fine-tuned and adjusted next time?

Once we are able to catch ourselves AFTER, DURING and BEFORE, that is when reliable transformation happens, because now we are aware, we are responding instead of reacting. Instead of looking at things and focussing on why they are not happening a certain way, we understand that things are happening the way they are and it is all meant for awakening. All of our experiences are parts of a precise curriculum designed for our awakening.

How do we activate the curriculum? We do this by surrendering to life without resistance. Whatever life may bring to us, we respond with 'thank you, thank you, thank you!' or 'bring it on, bring it on, bring it on!' We do this knowing that there are no mistakes in the universe. We simply welcome everything. The ego might hate it but if we are to grow and come into a greater awareness of our true nature, it is needed. In time, a beautiful transmutation happens and the separation that causes so much distress and friction in our lives gradually dissipates. A kind of transparency comes into our lives; we see ourselves not as separate from but as a part of this field of intelligence. An analogy would be that life is like a big sheet and while you can discern individual threads, the sheet itself is whole and complete in itself. We are all connected in this interwoven fabric of life. Gradually, we begin to see ourselves less and less as personalities and more and more as expressions of presence. We embody the trust that everything is in the right place.

To integrate our preparation with practice in our daily lives, we can simply begin to live more consciously. We do not have to wait for something unwanted to appear in our lives to practise. We can simply be in a state of awareness through the day and in time, even the strong distinctions between likes and dislikes, wanted and unwanted, the so called positive and negative experiences become less rigid. What remains is a state of flow, a spacious presence and a welcoming of all that is.

Here are some of my favourite mantras for conscious living. They remind me of some of the most important lessons I have learned in my journey.

1. Cancel: When limiting, complaining and 'virus' thoughts arise, simply say 'Cancel.'
2. How Wonderful: To welcome and appreciate whatever happens.
3. Thank You: When repeated many times, evokes a deep sense of gratitude.
4. Rule #6: Which means 'Don't take life so-ooo seriously!' And no, there are no other rules! Then, why is it called Rule #6? Don't take life so-ooo seriously!
5. Bring It On: The powerful mantra of a spiritual warrior who knows that all problems and challenges dissolve as soon as we welcome and embrace them.
6. *Mai Yur Ma:* An intention of pure, unconditional love made with the mind, words and actions by drawing a heart and infinity symbol (∞) with our hands or fingers, or even in our imagination.
7. Be Happy: An inner wish we generate when meeting anyone. Another version is 'I wish you happiness' or the Hindi phrase *'Sukhi Ho, Mangal Ho!'*, meaning may you be happy and well.
8. Is It True?: Evokes curiosity, wonder and the willingness to question our own and other people's thoughts and beliefs, which deepens our wisdom.

9. No One Owes Me Anything: A reminder that everyone is living in their own cute little world with their own cute little priorities and perspectives. No one owes us anything. We are the ones we have been waiting for.

10. Namaste: Which means, 'The highest in me bows to the highest in you.' It is also powerful to say the full translation to remind each other what this beautiful greeting means.

11. Another Me: Seeing others as essentially another me, just in the clothes of a different body, life story and belief system.

12. Channel of Blessings: Seeing oneself and all others as bright and beautiful channels of love, light and wisdom in this world.

13. Divinity in Clever Disguise: Seeing oneself and all others as God or Buddha or the benevolent intelligence of life in clever disguise, here to help each other grow and be free of our imaginary limitations.

14. And So It Is: This is the translation of the Sanskrit phrase *Tathaasthu!* which is said whenever anyone voices some heartfelt wish or intention. It's a way of saying may this truly happen for you.

15. This or Something Better: A great way to end all our intentions. It reminds us that sometimes not getting what we want may be the best as life has something even better planned for us. The full version is, 'This or something better happens in a joyful and harmonious way, at the right time, for the highest benefit of all!'

16. Tell Me More: The gateway words for deeper, more authentic and meaningful conversations and an indicator of the gift of deep listening. One can also say, 'Why is that important to you?' or simply, 'Say more.'

17. I See You: The first in the series of deep listening mantras. The others are, 'I hear you. I feel you. I love you. I am you. Thank you!'

18. Connection Before Correction: The most powerful principle in all relationships. It means to deeply understand and appreciate the other before trying to change or advise them in any way. For people do not care about what we say until they know how much we care.

19. Maybe You're Right, Maybe It's True: A good thing to say when we don't fully agree with someone but don't want to get into a big discussion either. It's also called agreeing to disagree.

20. Not This: The mantra that spontaneously arises when we know deep inside that a certain situation or relationship or occupation is no longer serving us. We may not know what to do next, but to honour this inner knowing can change our life forever.

21. Shenpa to Rigpa: Shenpa means stickiness or attachment and Rigpa means sky like, open awareness that is forever unaffected and free. Our whole journey is from Shenpa to Rigpa in all aspects of our life.

22. Not Knowing: An inner reminder and invitation to let go of assumptions, expectations and be 'agendaless'.

23. Bearing Witness: Entering into the other person's world and deeply empathizing with their unique thoughts, feelings, needs and challenges.

24. Loving Actions: Allowing love to shape our actions, not just thoughts and ideas of what might be helpful.

25. Fully Feeling: A reminder that fully feeling what we are feeling is very healing.

26. Infinite Patience: A reminder that nature never hurries, yet everything gets done at the right time and that infinite patience is the fastest way.

27. No Problems: Reminds us that in the present moment there are never any problems. Things just are as they are.

28. Life is One Continuous Mistake: A powerful lesson that invites us to embrace our foolishness and not be so attached and perfectionistic.

29. Relax! Nothing is under control: Realizing that ego grows through controlling and wisdom grows through observing things just the way they are.

30. Stardust: When we feel low, we remind ourselves that the matter in our body comes from an exploding star, so in a sense we are a star! When we feel too special, we remind ourselves that we are essentially just dust. So, the secret of life is Stardust!

14

On Grace

Who amongst us is so wise
that they can speak of what aches
within all of humanity
or what brings a child to his knees?
Who has held in the palm of his own hand,
the beating of each heart,
and known that it beats within each loss,
each trepidation,
or the languorous flight of hope?

Do we know with certainty
what makes a father bleed,
a mother awaken at the crack of dawn,
to sew by the light
of the breaking day,
until all of her is needle pricks,
the sky has fallen through her,
and yet she endures?

If there is something I do know,
and which no eyes can see,
or hands can touch,
it is this:

Through our darkest nights,
sometimes, we are carried,
though our hearts may be breaking,
sometimes, we are saved;
and is it love, is it grace,
we cannot name it or call it,
it comes as it pleases,
and when it departs,
we only know it had been there,
and we are better for it.

Trust the Process

Infinite patience is the fastest way

Does this happen to you? You experience something that touches you and the immediate impulse is: 'Who can I share this with?' The need to share our experiences seems to be part of our DNA. At a retreat or talk, it is common for people to come up to me and say: 'Someone I know really needed to hear this. I wish they were here today.' I smile and tell them: 'Actually, you need to hear this.' Whenever we think that someone else needs to learn something, usually it is something we need to learn. I also discovered that I teach others what I most need to learn myself. What really vexes us is not that others are not practising what we believe, but that we are not fully practising what we believe. It's fascinating that the outer world in some way is a reflection of our inner world. We need to trust the process.

I was exposed to the idea of trusting our process rather early. I went to a free progress school called Mirambika in New Delhi. At this school, students chose what they wanted to study. This was a radical experiment in trusting your process. I remember being asked, 'How come animals in nature know exactly what to do without ever going to school?' Nobody taught them. They just know it.

How is it that humans don't know? The thing is that we humans do know. We just never recognized, valued and allowed it. Children have two innate instincts— Imitation and curiosity. Every child imitates. Whatever you do, they imitate. I've read about a scientist who researched the mimicking ability of newborn children. She pulled up her nose as she looked at the child. The infant also started twitching his nose. Can you believe it? The little child twitching his nose? The second instinct is curiosity, which involves asking endless questions about every aspect of life.

At Mirambika, these two inborn capacities guided the entire educational process. Not only did we get to study what we wanted, we also got to evaluate ourselves. It made us honest about our own process. First, we identified why we wanted to study a certain topic. Then we went to the library to get the relevant books and then met teachers in school who knew more about those topics that we were interested in. After we finished our projects, we asked ourselves these questions in our self-evaluation: How did I do? Did I meet the objectives I had set for myself? What can I do better next time?

As for imitation, our teachers would join us in sports to set an example. If we were playing football and the teacher committed a foul, they would immediately raise their hand and say, 'My foul.' The teachers taught us integrity, not by preaching but by example. It didn't matter if the other players didn't see the foul or the referee missed it. If it was their mistake, they would own up. This created a culture of taking responsibility. If they were late for any class, even by a few minutes, they would apologize to the class, just like the students were expected to do.

We went on a school trip once when some kids got up to some mischief and one of the kids got caught. Now the teacher didn't know that there were other kids involved and the one kid who got caught was going to get admonished. I overheard the other kids saying: 'Listen, we all did it and he alone is going to get reprimanded. Let's all go and own up.' The kids didn't have to do that, but they wanted to play fair and all of them took responsibility. This is how my journey towards trusting my process began.

David Bohm, a famous physicist, in his book, *Wholeness and the Implicate Order* [13] examines if there might be a deeper underlying reality beneath space and time, an implicate order to our life? This is something mystics from all spiritual traditions have always pointed towards. What is it like to trust this implicate order? What is it like to tap into it? I believe that as we ripen in understanding, we begin to trust more. Maybe we do it through a spiritual process or a scientific process or just life experience, but we begin to trust a deeper order that guides our life. We learn to rest and relax into it.

When I lived as a forest monk, we learned to rely on the implicate order underlying our life. We couldn't always see the workings of this first hand, but we learned to trust it. It's not always visible, yet you learn to feel the invisible support of reality. So, we lived in a forest with all kinds of insects including a particular species of aggressive ants. These ants didn't just bite you, they injected a caustic irritant under your skin. So, you literally felt like you had received a strong electric shock and there was disbelief at how a tiny ant could have delivered such agony. There were also scorpions, snakes and occasionally larger animals as well. When you're living in that atmosphere where you don't have that much protection from the wild and the elements, you learn to rely on something deeper.

The Buddha says in his teachings that when we visit the wilderness, we have to remember that we are the guests and we must be respectful and mindful of the beings who have been there before us. Even in our prayers, monks prayed to all the beings in the forest saying: 'I've come here to practise. I don't want to disturb any of you and whatever goodness comes out of my practice, I will share the merits of that practice with all of you so that we coexist harmoniously.' The chant is known as the *Khanda Paritta*. The Buddha says that is a requirement for all practitioners who visit wilderness areas to recite it.

The prayer also gives us an inner feeling of confidence that we are here in loving kindness and a deep trust that we will not be harmed. So very rarely did we have a case of a monk getting bitten by a snake. And we've heard so many stories about spiritual teachers who have had close encounters with cobras, lions, tigers and all kinds of wild animals, but the teachers have come to no harm.

There's another fun story of a mouse that kept going into a monk's hut. Since monks are not allowed to kill any living creature, he meditated saying: 'Dear mouse, I'm sure you are really enjoying this hut. But if you don't mind, could you go somewhere else and not come here any longer?' He made that little intention and two days later, the mouse stopped visiting. Another monk got rid of termites in a similar manner. For many, this will sound unbelievable. I recommend you try connecting with the uninvited creatures in your home and lovingly requesting them to leave and see how it works.

Being in touch with the underlying intelligence of life is not something that is limited to monks or spiritual practitioners. Every one of us can find this connection. One way of knowing that this is happening is that synchronicities increase. We think of something and it shows up. This starts to happen very quickly, in a mirror-like way. We could also call this super accelerated living. The more in alignment we are, the more life starts to be smooth and just starts to flow. It's quite effortless.

I saw this happen with a family who lived in Troy in New York state. I was at their beautiful home, which was over a hundred years old. It was made of wood with a beautiful, big piano in one room. The family included all kinds of artists—one of them a writer, another a painter. A few months after I came back to India, I received a message that their house caught fire. There was a short circuit in their basement and since the house was made of wood, the whole house had caught fire. Of course, the fire services arrived and tried to put it out. But it was a big fire and the lady of the house just stood outside and began crying. Her friends held her as she was crying, but between her tears she was heard saying, 'I can't see it yet. I can't see it yet but I'm sure there's a blessing in this.' I was amazed when I heard this. The house is burning and you have the wisdom to say I can't see it yet, but I'm sure there's a blessing in this.

The family had an art exhibition planned the following month. Since Troy is a small town, news spread that their house caught fire. The family of artists were expecting a hundred people for the exhibition, but close to a thousand people showed up for the exhibition just to show solidarity. They not only attended the exhibition, but they made contributions. Everybody made small contributions or whatever they could afford. And one of their neighbours on the same street offered her house rent-free for the family to stay. So, on the one hand, watching their home go up in flames was a very unpleasant experience, but on the other hand, it led to a kind of connection and a community coming together like never before. The family's intention came true and a lot of blessings came out of that intention.

The language of this inner intelligence is not concepts, it's feelings. We may have been told not to trust our feelings as they are fleeting and unreliable. However, feelings have a tremendous intelligence of their own. A big part of trusting our process is learning to unpack the messages in these feelings.

I like to ask myself these questions when considering a decision: Does this make me feel more expanded or more contracted? Lighter or heavier? Does the path ahead seem clear or complicated? I have learned to trust the thoughts and decisions that make me feel more expansive, light and clear. Although in some cases I have needed to slow down and really notice my inner experience in a more nuanced way, I can say that such reflection and inner inquiry has served me well.

The main thing in trusting your process is patience. So don't be in such a rush, slow down. Notice that in nature, there is no hurrying. Nature does not rush and yet everything gets done. Human beings are constantly in a rush and there are always more things to be done. I wonder if any human has died with a fully checked-off to-do list.

Life has a voice of its own. Life has an impulse of its own. We can start to trust that impulse. We can honour that impulse and it will guide us. As we trust it, the right thing is said at the right time. With this inner compass, you'll have so many wonderful stories of your own to tell. This is the gateway to the most miraculous life. Every day is like a fresh adventure. This is my wish for you.

A Practice:

Take a nice, deep breath and just close your eyes. I want you to think of an example in your life, where you really trusted your process. It might've gone against conventional wisdom or what seemed like the obvious thing to do. Or what other people were recommending that you should do. But you went ahead and trusted something deeper, a deeper knowing inside yourself. You just trusted something, and you went out on a limb. You trusted something inside yourself. Remember what the process was like and what the result of that was like. Think of one clear example and just get comfortable with this question. Take one full minute. The memory will come to you by itself. It'll be great if you can just relax and let the memory surprise you as well.

And remember the details of what it was like? What was it like in that moment to trust? It could be a very simple incident. It could be a very simple example from school or college or any time in your life. Take a nice deep breath. Remain still and nourish the memory deep inside you. Just take it in.

Take another deep breath and open your eyes.

Section 3

A Deeper Playfulness

15

What Endures

The living flame
dies in one exhaled breath,
the pregnant rain cloud
dissolves to nothingness,
the morning chime of the temple bell
folds into the belly of a quiet afternoon,
the lone boy,
holding his mother's hand
turns the corner,
the lane is desolate again.

If witnessed,
by a man, a crow, a scratching dog,
they remain an imprint,
even if un-recalled
and if not,
if unseen, unheard, unfelt,
is there within this universe,
a remembrance,
that they too were a moment,
an infinitesimal birth,
that they too once,
were the stuff of this universe,

if only a bubble,

that rose and collapsed

into the infinite surface of being.

A Reflection on Death

Can we die to who we think we are?

A Zen Master was once asked, 'What happens after we die?' He replied, 'I don't know.' 'You don't know? You are a famous Zen Master! How can you not know?' He smiled and said, 'Yes, but not a dead one.'

Ajahn Chah, one of my teachers, said that for someone who has never contemplated death, life is very confusing. We see that in today's world as well—there is a lot of anxiety and dread. As we create some space to contemplate the only certainty there is—death—we begin to value each day as precious and each meeting as a holy encounter.

One way to know the maturity of our spiritual practice is by how taken aback or shocked we are when we hear that someone has passed on. Go through a newspaper, death is all around. And yet, when someone we know dies, there can be a sense of disbelief. Yet, this is the way it is. The Buddha encourages us to reflect on these five things everyday: 'I am subject to old age; I am subject to disease; I am subject to death; All that is mine, beloved and pleasing will become otherwise; I am heir to my actions and intentions.' This way of thinking is grounding and reminds us to not take anything for granted.

It was significant learning for me to realize that we don't lose anyone, we return them. This is because losing implies that we own them. Returning is based on the reality that all meetings end in partings. Everything and everyone is borrowed, including the elements in our body, only to be returned in due course.

Some of us imagine that we will die twenty, thirty or forty years from now. But what if we knew that we were going to die six months from now? What if we knew that we just had six weeks? Or six days? What about today? What would happen? Something would definitely shift. We would not take things for granted in the same way. There would be a radical shift in the way we perceive our own body. This is because death contemplation is also a kind of a life contemplation. Life and death are inextricably connected.

The last words spoken by the Buddha were— *Vayadhamma Sankhaara, Appamadena Sampadetha.* All conditioned states are subject to decay, be diligent in your practice. This teaching encourages us to understand impermanence, which is the main realization that cuts through the fear of death. In a universe where everything is changing, change itself is the only constant, and therefore, the most reliable refuge. This is the opposite of what one would expect. The more completely one embraces death, the more peace arises, the more vibrant life becomes. Try this now with me: Assume you will die in the next minute. Notice what this does to how alert you are and how vividly you experience everything. When I do this, I notice all sensory experiences are heightened, time seems to stand still and I am no longer as bound or limited by the body and mind.

When we practise in this way, we may sometimes judge ourselves and feel we are not striving enough. However, I have met many meditators, many who are committed to living with awareness, and they share similar things; if they have a near-death experience, in that moment, looking into the face of death, their being is very serene. This reassures them that their self-judgements are not always valid. The mind is a poor evaluator of our progress. When we assume nothing is happening is usually when we are growing the most. Unknown to us, the roots of our practice are finding their way deep into our being and transforming it in ways we may not fathom.

In our society, we are overly attached to life and overly repulsed by death. An example of this is the insistence on putting people on life support. Sometimes an ailing individual knows that their time has come, and they are willing to gracefully move on. On such an occasion, to forcibly extend their lives through artificial means is to resist what is, and this can put a huge strain on the individual, their family and their caregivers. Sometimes they are ready to transition but we are unable to let go. While there is value in preserving life, allowing for a graceful and dignified death also deserves loving attention.

As we meditate, our identity becomes more transparent and there is greater access to beingness. There is a shift from personality to presence. This is a kind of mini-death.

For a while, we die to who we think we are. Notice this: To be present to what you are reading and experiencing right now is to let go of everything you have ever read and experienced before, as well as all your projections about the future. This is a small letting go. In this way, these practices slowly yet surely, prepare us for death, the big letting go.

Viktor Frankl, an Austrian psychiatrist and Holocaust survivor recounted an incident in his book, *Man's Search for Meaning*. [14] An elderly man who once came to meet shared that since his wife of fifty years had tragically passed away in a war bombing, he no longer had a will to live. Every day was so hard without her. Viktor Frankl asked him, suppose it was the other way around, suppose he had died before her, would that have been better? The old man was quiet for a while. He then responded, 'It would have been very hard for her, because she was emotionally and practically dependent on me in so many ways. Actually, it would have been much harder for her.' This realization immediately changed his whole perspective. All the while he was only thinking about himself. He didn't consider how it would have been for her. So, if one of them had to go, it was just as well that she went first. It didn't take away the fact that his wife had passed, yet it gave a new meaning to his reality. He left with a calmer, more composed heart.

Byron Katie, in her book, *A Mind at Home with Itself*,[15] says 'death has a terrible reputation, but it's only a rumor'. It's not good advertising to talk about death. In my experience, however, it is fascinating that life is full of paradoxes. A large part of my own practice as a monk was contemplation of death. I find there is great benefit in demystifying death and examining it more intimately.

There are significant cultural differences in the way death is perceived and processed. Of course, when we lose a loved one, it is unsettling, but the understanding of death varies across traditions. For example, I lived in Thailand and I was amazed to find that when there was a cremation, the villagers came together, popular music was played, soft drinks were served and people would be chatting in a relaxed way. I discovered that in Thailand there is a constant reflection on death. It is a part of the Buddhist culture, so perhaps that makes them more accepting of it. They are able to process the departure of their loved ones in a calmer way. Undoubtedly, they too feel the pain of losing someone dear, yet from what I witnessed, they are not as heavy and solemn about it. A lot of our reactions and behaviours are connected very intimately to the meaning we give to them. Grief and grieving, while natural, is also a culturally learned response.

What we define as 'me', is usually the body and mind, but this 'me' is changing all the time. Anything that we are aware of, that we can experience or perceive is not ourselves. We tend to misidentify ourselves with our thoughts and feelings and sensory experiences. The reality is that these things are arising, passing and changing constantly. How can something which is constantly in flux be considered as a stable and enduring 'me'? So, the process of inquiry is a process first of negation. I am not this chair, because 'I' am aware of this chair. I am not this hand, because 'I' am aware of this hand. I am not these feelings, because 'I' am aware of these feelings. It is the same with thoughts and everything else. In the end, what we are left with is undefinable, indescribable and thereby not subject to birth and death. We touch our essence in this way and this essence reveals itself to be empty of all attributes, and thereby, capable of freely and fluidly containing all polarities of existence. Simultaneously, I am revealed to be nothing and everything and something. In this triple recognition, there is a peace and freedom that is not limited in any way. This is what frees us from the fundamental fear of death. Now there may be a habit of personality that clings to form, feelings and identities, but it cannot overwhelm us anymore. Our foundation is clear and unobstructed.

I have had the opportunity to bear witness to very conscious deaths. None of us know how we are going to die and my understanding is that we cannot die, because whatever will die will not be us, in a larger sense. In the meantime, let us live excellently, love excellently and let us depart excellently. Let all of it be done playfully, joyfully and with a sense of humour. There are ways to help us prepare; in the way of daily practices, embracing our own mortality and living each moment as if it were our last.

A Practice:

This practice first came to me in Lumbini, where the Buddha was born. It is a powerful invitation for letting go. We begin with the assumption that we know our life is about to end.

We have ten minutes left in this lifetime. Since we know that we only have ten minutes left, a tremendous process of letting go begins, a tremendous process of putting things down begins. There is no need to hold on to stuff anymore. It is time to really let go. Tremendous alertness comes. In this practice, use the phrase, 'I am dying to' or 'I let go of'. Some examples being: I am dying to all the ways that I have judged myself and others. I am dying to my fear and hesitation around death. I choose to enter whatever comes willingly. I am dying to any regret, any unfinished business, any lingering sense of incompleteness, I am dying to all of this, I am completely letting it go.

And now, in the next two minutes or so, assume that physical death is coming, complete death is coming. So, accelerate this process of letting go and merge into your own essence and rest there for a bit. Let go completely. So, practise the state of being that you would like to have as you approach death. Practise the state of being now. Allow yourself to merge into the great unknown, fully trusting, fully letting go. For a moment, forget everything.

As it turns out, it was not actually death, it was just a near-death experience. Now, use the phrase 'I now choose', since death has not yet come and there is still life, still time. Now let the nudges and whispers of existence find you. Complete the sentence: The new reality I'm stepping into is . . .

16

Pause

To look left
when the whole world
seems to be grasping at your chin,
to look right;
is a moment claimed

They want you to react,
sympathize,
peer into your eyes,
and comfort,
themselves, confirm,
yes, you are one of us

You must loudly,
publicly beat your chest,
mark your protest,
outrage, outrage,
exactly like everybody else

In this race,
can there be space,
or a pause,
a pause, to grieve, reflect,

or must we constantly deflect,
away, away from self

Why,
why must I comply,
my heart will sometimes ache,
sometimes fly,
or be unsure, or wonder why,
so, no.

What moves me will find expression,
or not,
you will hear my voice, my
consternation,
or not,
I will conform,
or not.

Speak to Improve upon the Silence

The transformational power of pause

Imagine this: You are walking on the beach in a straight line, keeping about the same distance from the sea. You notice that most waves come close enough but recede, but around every seventh wave is a much larger wave. It washes your feet before going back. This pattern keeps repeating itself. Each time it feels like you are far enough for the wave to not reach you, but it does and then recedes. This is how the ocean heaves and breathes. Please take a minute to think about this image and contemplate what it means to you.

Let me share my interpretation. There is a constant impulse in us to speak. I am reminded of the Quakers' concept of 'speak if you must speak'. For instance, there may be an urge within me to speak but it's a small wave and I let it pass. The next one is another small wave and I let it pass. Likewise, the big wave may not be a numerical seven, but can I wait until there is a big wave of something that wants to be expressed?

For instance, you are with people and you feel a wave rise within; there is a desire to share some trivia or something funny. You notice it and let it pass. Another wave arises. You let it pass. You only really speak when you are moved to speak. It is important to get a sense of what really needs to be said. Not everything that arises needs to be said. Every thought or impression or opinion need not be shared. For example, you may be a naturally witty person but sometimes your wit may unknowingly take precedence over sensitivity. The comment might not be appropriate or timely.

We can bring awareness to this notion at a level deeper than speech by extending the same principle to our actions. In his book, *I Am That*, [16] Nisargadatta Maharaj says, 'The steady resistance to the unnecessary is the secret of success'. Often, we get drawn into all kinds of unnecessary activities and projects. However, if we just waited for the seventh wave, perhaps we could be far more conscious of our thoughts and actions. There is a Native American saying:

When you make a decision, can you consider its impact on the seventh generation? We speak to improve upon the silence. As we can be mindful of our speech, our actions too must not cause disturbance in the present or in the future.

Bhagwan Ramana Maharshi's ashram has a communal dining hall where people line up to receive their food. One of his students was very quiet; he hardly ever spoke but he had a tremendous presence. Once all the students were in line and there was a lot of chatter. This student, who was generally silent, merely stepped out of the line and raised his hand. With his one gesture, the entire line fell silent. He didn't need to say a word. He simply stepped out of the line and raised his hand. That was the power of his presence.

The seventh wave analogy can be one way of thinking about what truly drives or moves us. Words and actions are not orphans. They have a parentage. Behind our words and actions are the waves of thoughts. Every little idea and thought need not find expression in words or actions. Instead of being swept away by every single one of them, we could wait to tune into what is really in harmony with a particular situation and with our inner guidance.

Perhaps the greatest transformational tool is simply the power of pause. When something happens, just pause. When you don't pause, that's called reaction. Why is it called reaction? Because it's a 're-enact-tion'. What you have done before, you just do that again, what you said before, you'll just say that again. If you pause, the appropriate response usually finds us.

As we pause, we can also reflect on the Three Gates of Speech. The first gate is: Is it true? If it's not true we stop there, and if we're not sure, we can say, 'I'm not sure this is true, but this is what I've heard,' and that is acceptable because that is true. The second gate is: Is it kind? Just because something is true doesn't mean we have to say it. There are some people who say with some pride that they always 'tell it as it is,' or 'don't mince words' and they do not realize that in the process they may actually crush someone's spirit or hurt their feelings. So, we must ask this of ourselves, is it kind? The truth is that for people to really be transformed, the truth must be delivered in the right way and at the right time, with compassion. Often it is how we say things and not just what we say that makes a difference. There is an astute saying, 'I can't hear what you're saying because who you are is too loud!'

The third gate of speech is, 'Is it necessary?' This is a powerful question which can lead to instant clarity. Is it necessary for me to say this? Do I really have to say this? In the world of economics, that which is abundantly available has low value. What is scarce has high value. If we apply the same principles to speech, if we are speaking all the time, without being mindful or circumspect, we devalue our words. However, if our speech is more considered, more economical, and we pause and then speak, there is a greater likelihood that our words will be heard and valued.

Even after we establish that what we are about to say is true, kind and necessary, it is wise to reflect on how it can be said. How can it be communicated in the kindest possible way? If we were to publicly call out someone, however well-intentioned we may be, would that really create a change? We could put ourselves in their shoes and ask, 'What would it take for this person to receive this?' People are most receptive when they are given space to be and they feel a level of trust. It is interesting that when we let go of the immediate urge to speak, and just wait, often people learn their own lessons. We must be aware of our deep desire to fix others, change their behaviour to what we find acceptable or useful. There is wisdom in letting people, especially children, learn their own lessons in their own time.

Richard Gere, a renowned actor was inspired by the Dalai Lama and became a Buddhist. The Dalai Lama treated him with a lot of love and kindness, and Richard was completely in awe of him. A few years later, however, the Dalai Lama began criticizing certain behaviours of his that he did not think were beneficial. Sometimes, he would even criticize him in front of other people. This confused Richard because he couldn't understand why the teacher who was so kind to him in the beginning was now criticizing him. However, he was still able to receive his censure because over the years, the Dalai Lama had built a strong foundation of trust. This demonstrates another powerful axiom: **Connection before Correction.**

Sometimes simply showing up is of greater value than what we say or do. The real gift is our undistracted presence. With meditative practices, it is possible to uncover a deep reservoir of inner silence. A place where you wonder if you really need anything at all. What do I need to get? What do I need to give? When you search within, you find that you need nothing, and you are willing to give everything. Your presence conveys, 'I am here, what do you need? Anything that I have is yours.' There is an openness and freedom in being in this state. Like breath which nourishes us while remaining invisible and expecting no recognition for itself, our presence quietly supports a fuller expression and experience of the moment. The desire to share with others doesn't arise from compulsiveness. Even our needs start to feel like: 'Wouldn't it be nice if . . .' There is no longer the heaviness of: 'I must have . . .' It can be a revelation to discover that the real gift is the gift of presence. Nothing needs to be said. Our silent presence is enough.

There is something I learned from the Authentic Relating and Circling movement which I find helpful. There are three kinds of conversations that we can have— Informational, Personal and Relational. Informational conversations operate at the level of facts or data. For instance, 'Which train should I take to get to a particular place?' or 'What's the weather today?' or 'Where do you live?' Typically when we first meet someone, the conversations are more informational in nature. We don't go beyond a certain point of superficial or need-based sharing of information. Of course, there is a place for that. We may not want to get into a deep conversation with everyone we meet. There is a time and a place for everything, so the first conversation is information.

The second is personal. At this level of engagement, not only do we share facts, we also share our feelings. We share stories of our lives, the challenges, the difficulties, the successes. As we get to know people better, we notice more details about them; we get a deeper understanding of their opinions, beliefs and personalities.

People are generally familiar with the first two kinds of conversation—informational and personal. Informational conversations are transactional. 'Who is picking up the kids tomorrow?', 'Have you booked the tickets?' Even with personal conversations, after a point, most stories, incidents and life experiences have been shared. So, if these are the only two levels of conversation, our friendships and relationships may begin to lose their sparkle and their freshness, leaving us feeling unfulfilled and uninspired.

Let us now discuss relational conversations. In such conversations, what we are essentially exploring is: 'What is alive in me as I'm with you right now.' Most of us are not used to speaking in this way. To be able to speak relationally requires speaking from presence. For instance, when I meet an old friend I haven't met in a while, the conversation need not be limited to generally catching up. This is an opportunity to share how I am experiencing being with this friend in this moment. I could say for example, 'As I'm with you there is a wonderful feeling of warmth and nostalgia. I feel like there are so many things I want to say all at once. I don't even know where to begin! I'm just so happy that you're here with me.' This is an example of a relational conversation.

Once I was with a group of people and they were speaking in a way that was hard for me to relate to. There was an energy of arrogance, of knowing it all that was grating. An example of a relational conversation in this context would be, 'As I hear you speak, a part of me is not able to connect with you. It just seems like you're so clear about everything and there's just no room for any other opinion. Can you help me understand you better?'

This takes a certain amount of authenticity and it can be scary. There could be a sharp reaction but we have to be mindful of our words. We do not go and say, 'What's wrong with you? You're so stuck up and so full of yourselves!' Instead, we say: 'This is what is alive in me right now. Help me out, I'm actually not able to connect to what you're saying.' It takes skill and practice. As long as we can share our reality, without expressing judgement, there is space for authentic connection. The moment I attach a label, there will be defensiveness. As long as we can keep our judgement on hold and share what is alive in us at that moment, the person being spoken to will likely pause for a moment and think about what we said. This can create a space that leads to a deeper, more authentic conversation.

Relational conversations are like meditation. It is about being in tune with oneself and the other and the context. Meditation is being attentive to what's happening right now. Such attentive noticing and sharing can be brought into conversation. The more we practise this, the more we notice Shenpa coming up. What is Shenpa? Shenpa is a Tibetan word for stickiness. Have you noticed that certain thoughts are sticky and certain feelings are sticky. You keep thinking about them over and over again, 'How could that person say that?', 'How could that person do that?', 'Why did that happen to me?' The more sticky it is, the more Shenpa there is.

The opposite of Shenpa is Rigpa. Rigpa is like the open sky, it's like the open mind. In the sky nothing sticks, no matter what weather, no matter what bird, no matter what plane, no matter what cloud, no matter what storm—nothing sticks, they just move through. That's Rigpa, that's like our original mind, original state—no matter what happens in your life, it moves through. So, how do we shift from Shenpa to Rigpa? We become aware when Shenpa is rising in us, we pause between stimulus and response, we authentically connect and speak our truth, and we welcome whatever happens with 'How Wonderful!' This dissolves all stickiness.

A Practice:

Be aware of the Three Gates of Speech in all your interactions and conversations today.
Is it true? is it kind? Is it necessary?
Observe what arises within you before, during and after you have spoken. Reflect on what patterns you notice while being mindful of your speech.

17

On Liking

I like awkward people,
who haven't had their rough edges
sandpapered out of them into a
pleasing smoothness.

I like people with sharp edges who
catch more than most, and a tongue
that is innocent of fear or convention.

I like the dreamers, the ones who chew
on pencil stubs, and wear mismatched
socks and plan the next revolution.

I like the doers whose hands go ahead
of them, instinctive helpers who sleep
well at night after a good day's work.

I like the thinkers who disappear in the
middle of a crowded room, because a
strand of what they read is waiting for
them to unpack. They are, because they
think.

I like the comics with sadness in their
eyes, who find meaning in a four-year
old helpless with laughter rolling on the
floor.

I like the lovers, who paint the sky each
night in the colours of their desire, and
sleep with a poem on their breath, only
to awaken the next morning,
with a memory and a sleepy scribble into a
worn notebook.

I like myself, and all the parts that do not
fit, that are disobedient, that love
fiercely and sometimes quietly. They
dance and write and show up for things
and people and school and parties and
for that friend who wants to talk when I need
to be alone, writing, writing, writing.

I like many people and don't think too
much about the ones I don't.

Enjoyment without Modification

Be here now

A participant in one of my sessions once shared an
interesting experience. Just out of curiosity he visited

a Tibetan monastery in Karnataka. While there, he wondered about meditation. He approached an old monk who seemed wise and experienced and asked him, 'Can you please teach me how to meditate?' The monk didn't speak English very well and only spoke Tibetan. However, he understood his question and wanted to help him, so he held his hand and led him to a hill behind the monastery.

They spent an hour climbing, until they reached a large, flat rock on the top of the hill. The monk asked him to sit. Before them was a breathtaking expanse that stretched all the way to the horizon. The monk looked at him with a toothless smile and said, 'Enjoy!' and then he walked away. Our man was thoroughly confused and thought to himself, 'What am I supposed to do now?' He thought they had come here to meditate and yet the only instruction he had been given was 'Enjoy!' Three hours later the monk returned and led him back down the hill.

The participant told me that those three hours changed his life. He found that the simple experience of being by himself on that hill had put him in touch with something precious—being present and comfortable in his own skin. From being someone who was always restless at work, he became more composed. While the usual stresses of work remained, he became more spacious within and was even able to enjoy himself. When he was with his family, he was more relaxed, calm and happy. Turns out, the monk has taught him the essence of meditation with just a one-word instruction: 'Enjoy!'

Can you be comfortable in your own skin? At the end of all our study of philosophy and religion, if we have not learnt to be comfortable in our own skin, we have missed the point of it all. To simply enjoy being by and with yourself can be an invaluable learning. It may sound simple but it can be one of the most challenging things to practise.

I define meditation as an intimate meeting with oneself. We meet others our whole lives, so how about for once, you just meet yourself? An intimate meeting with yourself is a meeting without judgements. Is it possible for you to meet yourself without judgement?

When I began meditating, I would catch myself thinking, I can't do this, there's too much on my mind, I feel restless and impatient. I would judge and resist my experience much of the time. This is how I came out of this pattern. I asked myself: If I had to meet a close friend, would I call him and say, 'I will meet you provided you make me feel calm, peaceful and happy.' If I did this, I imagine my friend would say, 'Why can't we just meet? Why add these prerequisites? It feels stressful to have to meet such demands. Why not just meet to be with each other, you as you are and I as I am.' When you meet yourself, try to meet yourself without conditions and simply enjoy whatever arises, without likes and dislikes, without strong ideas of how it should be, how it could be. So, the recognition that helped me heal my relationship with meditation was letting go of expectations that I needed to be a particular way. I now refer to meditation as an 'agendaless' presence.

As we begin to practise, we notice that no matter how difficult our meditation is, at the end of the meditation, we always feel a little bit more clear-headed, a little bit lighter, a little bit calmer. One lifelong lesson I can offer you regarding meditation is this: Whatever happens in meditation is good! Whether it is pleasant or unpleasant, calming or confronting, boring or exhilarating, it's all good. Why? Because it is revealing that all experiences come and go, and so our primary identity shifts from identification with thoughts and feelings to simply observing and being.

Our lives are often an endless stream of calculations. If I do this, I will get that. Before I invest time or energy in anything, I must be sure of the benefit. How much should I give and how much will I receive in return? This mindset is not restricted to material things. It even spills into our relationships. All aspects of life can become shallow and transactional. Meditation is an invitation to step away and experience a new way of being. Just like we meet close friends—just to meet them, with no hope for gain or advantage—can we meet ourselves as well without any expectations? We practise for no reason, not even for peace. We practise for the sake of practice. Would you be willing for meditation to be that one sacred part of your life which is approached without any calculation?

Just for a little while, could we try non-modification, non-resistance and non-judgement and not try to change even one per cent of this moment? It is just as it is. Ask yourself: 'Can I for once in my life try not to modify this moment?'

The idea is to be comfortable in our own skin, comfortable in our own feelings and comfortable in our own thinking. It does not have to be perfect. Happiness is not about perfection. It is about connection. Don't seek perfection in your life because this search is without end. No matter where you arrive, there is always going to be more.

I have had many intentions, dreams and desires in my own life and so many of them actually got fulfilled. It is possible that you too have had dreams and desires that came true for you. Yet today they have been replaced with different dreams and desires. So, you see it is a never-ending cycle. Can you see how your mind entraps you? Would you be willing to call its bluff? Can we go from something has to change for me to be happy to nothing has to change for me to be happy?

I once heard a story about the Dalai Lama who was in Australia addressing a conference and he was part of a panel that included some eminent people—a senior professor of a university, a well-known author, an important head of state and so on. All of these luminaries were engrossed in an animated discussion but the Dalai Lama wasn't talking much and was mostly quiet through the proceedings. Towards the end of the event, the facilitator announced that there were only five minutes left. He posed one last question to each of the panellists: 'If there was one thing you would change in the world for the happiness of all, what would it be?' A panellist responded by saying he would end child malnutrition. Another chose to end gender discrimination. Everyone on the panel identified something in the world that urgently needed to change. When it was the Dalai Lama's turn, he said that he wouldn't change anything and that nothing needed to change for us to be happy.

How could he say nothing needs to change for us to be happy? Here is a man who has experienced so much upheaval and turmoil in his lifetime. He lives in exile and still asserts that nothing needs to change for us to be happy. This is a profound teaching. Even more so coming from a person who has experienced as much loss as he has. If he can say this, then certainly you and I can also begin to see life this way.

A lady who didn't understand any English, once came for my session. I noticed that she sat quietly through the entire duration of two hours. At the end of the session, I asked her, 'What was it like for you, since you don't speak any English?' Someone translated this to her. She said that it was just so peaceful. 'I didn't understand what you said, I felt it. I received everything I needed just by being here, by looking at everyone's faces and enjoying the energy in the room. I feel so happy and content,' she replied. Simply by being present, without a desire to modify the experience, without resistance, she benefited so much. It was almost as if she received more from the session by bypassing the words and connecting directly to the essence of what was being shared.

In this manner, we learn how to go through life without flinching, without turning away and without hardening ourselves. We are just open, open to life. Right now, take a couple of minutes and just get in touch with the part of you which is happy for no reason and is not in opposition to anything in the universe. For a couple of minutes, be quiet, be with yourself. If you like, you can say this aloud or in your heart: 'I choose to be happy for no reason. No one has to change. Nothing has to change for me to be at peace with this moment.'

Even after years of practice, I cannot claim to accept myself one hundred per cent. If we are not careful, perfection itself becomes an unattainable mirage that we chase. I have come to recognize that more important than perfection is connection. Can we accept ourselves as we are? Is self-acceptance quantifiable? Do we know how much self-acceptance we need to accumulate to be worthy in our own eyes? Isn't this also the myth of when—a very clever myth of when; when I have more self-acceptance, I will be happy. It sounds good, but it is a lie. The reality is that you accept yourself as much as you accept yourself.

A Practice:

Ramana Maharshi, a revered sage, said, 'My real teaching is my silence. I speak for those who do not understand this. The primary language is the language of silence.'

Today let's look beyond the words. Let's not just try to learn the concepts—let's try to touch it, feel it, know it. If it resonates it stays with you, you don't need to memorize it; it just stays with you. So, start with a few moments of gratitude and tune in to what we are grateful for.

Enjoy the sounds you are hearing.

Enjoy the breath, it is always there.

Enjoy feelings, they could be pleasant or unpleasant, just experience them the way they are.

Enjoy thoughts. Perceive them like clouds in a timeless sky.

Just be still and enjoy yourself. Conclude saying, 'How wonderful!'

18

The Deepest Yes

In stealth, He strides
across your darkness.
He comes to destroy
what does not serve you.
Only whisper,
welcome, welcome.

Empty Yourself of Yourself

Mind becomes feeling and body becomes light

A poet with an interest in mysticism was once very sick, to
the point where he nearly lost consciousness. In that state he
felt the mysteries of the universe had been revealed to him.
In his delirium, he determined it was important to write
down the essence of his experience so he would remember
it later. Next morning, he eagerly looked for what he had
written, and scribbled in barely legible handwriting were
the words, 'Flush the toilet!'

This is a humorous anecdote but perhaps, this is the
great truth—keep flushing it, keep flushing it. Why are we
holding on to that shit from years ago? Flush it, flush it.
Let it go. Let it go. Let it go. Keep moving. So, something

fascinating for me is that the more I empty myself, the more available I am to the source, the spirit and to the intelligence of the now. The more space there is within, the more I am the mouthpiece for what needs to be said, or maybe not said. So, I encourage everyone to play with this. It's very interesting, in your own field, in whatever that you do. Some of us are creative people, some are business people and we can bring this idea there. Presence implies absence. The more you empty yourself of agendas, limiting beliefs and fixed ideas, the more available you become to intuition and to guidance.

As you practise, two beautiful things happen—mind becomes feeling and body becomes light. Say this aloud or in your mind: 'Mind becomes feeling and body becomes light.' What does it mean? Mind becomes feeling. Instead of being caught up in cognition all day long—thinking, thinking, thinking—start feeling. Thinking is fine. Thinking is needed, but it is not necessary every minute of the day.

Feeling is the doorway to intuition. There are three kinds of feelings—pleasant, unpleasant and neither pleasant nor unpleasant, which is neutral, or a feeling that cannot be defined. The Buddha says when it is pleasant, we have a tendency to hold on to it. We want more and more of it because we like it. We get hooked. When it is unpleasant, we have a tendency to push it away. We don't like it, so we don't want it. If it keeps happening, there's a very strong aversion and irritation. The third one is neither pleasant nor unpleasant. This tends to create boredom or restlessness.

We unconsciously try to escape these neutral feelings with distractions and various ways to preoccupy ourselves.

There's a story about a man who is convicted and put in a prison and forced to live in a very confined space. The country he was in had such a large prison population that jails intended for short-term confinement were now being used for long-term imprisonment. There were people who didn't see the sky for years. This prisoner faked a tooth problem and complained about it repeatedly. Why? So that he would be taken out of his tiny cell and he could get a glimpse of the sky. The prisoner risked being called out on his bluff and perhaps even some form of harsher punishment, just to see the sky. When was the last time you and I felt such gratitude just to see the sky?

The Buddha said something very striking. He talked about suffering and explained how we all suffer. In essence, we suffer because we hold onto things. In a universe that is based on change, if we hold onto anything, we stay in the world of suffering. According to the Buddhist universe, we have a cosmology—there are human beings and below human beings, there exists an animal realm below which is the ghost realm, followed by the hell realm. There is also a *Deva* realm for the Gods and *Brahmic* realms. And some of these Brahmas have been around for so long that they have witnessed entire universes being born and collapsing, just like we open and close a book. In front of the Maha Brahma, thousands of universes have opened and collapsed, but the Brahma doesn't realize that he too is impermanent. The Buddha says that there is no greater suffering in the entire *Samsara*, than that of a Brahma who has begun to fade. This is because he assumed he was eternal and now he realizes he is also subject to impermanence and will be back in the spinning wheel of *Samsara*.

The reason we practise emptying ourselves is because anything that we try to hold onto, anything that we try to make our foundation will slip beneath our feet. So, get comfortable for a little while with having no coordinates. Having no foundation is unsettling in the beginning, but as you go along, it's got the best taste. A tasteless taste. Let me tell you a story. A group of visitors came to our monastery and a monk was assigned to show them around. One of them asked him how long it took him to clean his hut and he said it took him about fifteen minutes a day. She confessed she was envious since she spent her whole day overseeing the staff who cleaned her mansion. This simple anecdote leads to a powerful question: 'At what point do I stop owning things and things start owning me?'

A Sufi is generally known to be comfortable in the most modest dwelling, wearing ordinary clothing and valuing the simple life. However, when the Sufi is called to meet a king, he gets the higher seat. Nothing less than the finest food and clothing will do. The best of the best is offered to the Sufi. For when he meets the king, he is the representative of the Divine. In other words, while the Sufi is not attached to the story that he is a mendicant, he is also not attached to the story that if he wears expensive clothes, he is materialistic. The opposite of spiritual is not material. The opposite of spiritual is holding on tight to any kind of identity. Clinging to identities is the realm of egoic fixation.

Spirituality is shedding all of these identities, layer by layer. If we get attached to the identity of being a spiritual teacher, it's a really sticky and dangerous one. We can get very attached to the idea of being a teacher. Then we are in trouble because everywhere we go, we'd want to teach something. It takes a lot of attention to be aware of this. When I am with people, I need to let go of the need to give advice. People are capable of figuring things out by themselves. Yet, if I am called to, I can share my thoughts. Holding your identity lightly rather than being hung up about it is a continuous process of putting down. As the tree sheds all its leaves, the stars and the moon become visible. You have to die to who you think you are to be born to who you really are. When you plant a seed, it splits open. That can seem like a catastrophe. Yet it's the beginning of a new form. The seed has to die as a seed to become a tree. And the tree has to die to being a tree to become rich manure.

There is a lovely story of an archer who comes to the village square and starts shooting. In his first attempt, he hits the bull's eye. The villagers applaud. He shoots another arrow that cuts through the first arrow. Someone in the crowd says that it's just practice. Again, he shoots and it cuts open the second arrow. A villager again says that it's just practice. The archer repeats the feat three or four times, and finally just gets irritated and asks the village what he means by 'just practice'. He asks the villager if he could shoot the arrows like he could. The villager comes out of the crowd and says to the archer, 'I'm not trying to undermine you but let me show you something.'

He holds an empty bottle with a small mouth in one hand. In his other hand is a bottle filled with oil. He holds the oil bottle high up and pours the oil into the other bottle. Not a single drop is spilled. He turns to the archer and asks if he could do what he just did. The archer responds that he couldn't and that it looked really tough. The villager says that he is the son of an oil merchant. 'Since my childhood, I have been pouring oil. Now, after years of practice, I can do it easily. You have also been practising your skill and that's why you can do it.'

The idea of this story is this: We are practising something all the time. The most basic thing we are practising is dispersing and distracting ourselves or collecting ourselves. There are a million places to disperse ourselves just as there are many wholesome places we can collect ourselves. The choice remains with us.

Being dispersed and frazzled has a particular taste. In the same way, being in a state of openness and presence also has a distinctive state. It is the taste of truth, the taste of purification. In this state, it will not occur to you to ask the purpose of your life. Those questions do not arise in that state, because you are your life. Life is then breathing and living through you. Such questions only arise when you are distracted and looking at other people's lives and wondering, 'What is the purpose of my life?'

A useful exercise is to stop and ask ourselves: 'What am I practising?' Are we practising jealousy, anger, sadness and manipulation? Is this really what I want to practise? Let us become mindful of that. Once we are mindful of what is going on within us, it becomes easier to set things down and to not hold onto feelings, identities and assumptions so tightly. This creates a natural space and ease, to come into who we really are, and allows us to live our lives intuitively, joyously and creatively.

A Practice:

Let's do a small exercise. Close your eyes for a moment. In your mind's eyes, visualize a large beautiful tree that makes you feel happy. You may have already seen it or it may be an imaginary tree. It is alright. You find yourself getting drawn to a particular branch and a particular leaf on this tree.

Check the shape and colour of the leaf. Suddenly, you discover that you have gone so close to the leaf that you have become this leaf.

Now you are gently swaying in the wind. Sunlight falls on you, night arrives, different seasons come and go. Around you are other leaves, they may be your family members. Further away are friends and acquaintances, leaves you have seen and know a little about. Still further away are leaves you know nothing about.

Quite unexpectedly, a day comes when you find yourself detaching from your stem. Now you are floating. You are free floating, twisting left and right. The sky and trees and ground are alternating in your awareness. You come all the way down and settle on the ground. You see a big tree and the sky above you. You relax. Slowly, you find yourself dissolving and disintegrating and becoming one with the soil.

From the soil, the root network of not just this tree but all the trees in this forest absorbs you. You realize that you are now the forest. The forest realizes that it's part of a planet. The planet realizes that it's part of a galaxy. The galaxy realizes it is part of the universe and infinity. You had to become a leaf to be born as a soil, tree, forest and the universe.

Take a slow deep breath. Rub your palms together. Bring them over your eyes. Open your eyes slowly.

19

The Search

You know that time,
when you went into the mountains,
and offered your sunken belly to the gods,
your matted hair and bare feet,
a penance to empty all of human desire
into the earthen pot of a *bhikshu,*
did you feel him then?

And when you,
the lonely student of music,
traversed deep
into the heart of a single note,
and it revealed to you a universe
you could not explain to a jostling crowd
in a highway bus, your headphones
a bridge to another world,
did you hear him then?

and you, with the bleeding feet,
disfigured in pursuit
of the perfect movement in ballet,
in that moment when there is
no dance and no dancer,
no music, no audience,

only a moment of exquisite beauty,
did he dance in you then?

and you, the professor of advanced mathematics,
staring at your whiteboard late into the night,
unfed, unbathed,
wide eyed at the poetry of an equation
so breathtaking in its simplicity,
in what has always been,
did you find him then?

and you and I,
in our everyday ordinariness,
in our tired shoulders, our aching feet,
our one more day and one more night,
in the embers of our dreams,
in the flights of our desires,
in the voices of our children,
in the soft whispers of our lovers,
in the promise of a blushing dawn,
in the stillness of a placid moon,
do we still seek to find him then?

and if we do, will we know that it is he,
who lies beyond all seeking,
beyond our maze of thoughts and feelings,
beyond our pursuits and goals
and all manners of wanting?

Will we then be home?

Liberation through Surrender

When strong, serve. When weak, surrender.

One of the great Sufi Masters, Junayd, was dying. A close disciple approached him and softly asked, 'Master, you are leaving us. We have learned so much from you, however, one question has always been on our minds. Who was your teacher? We have always had this great curiosity but we could never gather the courage to ask you.' Junayd opened his eyes and said, 'It will be difficult for me to answer because I have learned from almost everybody. All of existence has been my teacher. I have learned from every event that has happened in my life. I am grateful to all that has happened, it has all been a blessing.'

Junayd went on to say, 'To satisfy your curiosity I will give you three instances. Once I was very thirsty and I went towards the river carrying my begging bowl, the only possession I had. When I reached the river, a dog came running, jumped into the river and started drinking. I watched the dog for a moment and threw away my begging bowl as I realized I had no use for it anymore. Even a dog could do without it. I too jumped into the river and drank water to my heart's content. I sat in the river for a few moments, thanked the dog and bowed before him with great reverence because he had taught me a valuable lesson. I reflected on how I had dropped everything, all possessions, but there was a certain clinging to my begging bowl. It was a beautiful bowl, very beautifully carved, and I was always aware that somebody might steal it. Even at night, I would put it under my head as a pillow so nobody could snatch it away. That was my last attachment. It was so clear: I was always taken care of even with little or no possessions. I simply needed to trust the intelligence of life and know that my needs would be met. That dog was one of my teachers.

On another occasion, I lost my way in a forest and by the time I reached the nearest village it was midnight. Everybody was fast asleep. I wandered all over the village to see if I could find shelter until finally, I found one man. "Can you give me shelter for the night?" I asked. The man replied, "From your gown I can tell that you are a Sufi monk." The man said, "I am perfectly willing to give you shelter, but I must tell you who I am. I am a thief. Would you like to be the guest of a thief?" Taken aback, Junayd hesitated. The thief said, "You seem reluctant. How strange that the thief is willing but the mystic seems to be hesitant to enter the house of a thief. I should be afraid of you. You may change me, you may transform my whole life! But I am not afraid. You are welcome. Come to my home and stay as long as you want. However, you still seem unsure.'" Junayd realized that the thief's words were true. Immediately he asked to be forgiven.

He said, 'You're right. I apologize for my hesitation. I would like to accept your invitation.' The thief led him to his house, made sure he was comfortable and said, 'Now I must go. I have my work to do. I will come back early in the morning.' When he returned the next morning, Junayd asked, 'Have you been successful?' The thief said, 'No, not today, but I will see tomorrow.' This continued for thirty days; every night the thief went out, and every morning he came back empty-handed. But he was never sad or frustrated. There was no sign of failure on his face and he always seemed happy. He would say, 'It doesn't matter. I tried my best. I could not find anything today again, but tomorrow I will try. Inshallah, it can happen tomorrow if it has not happened today.' Soon Junayd left, and for years he tried to realize the ultimate, but success eluded him. However, each time he decided to give up, he remembered the thief, his smiling face and his attitude of surrender. Junayd continued, 'I remember the thief as one of my greatest teachers. Without him I would have given up a long time ago.'

Junayd recounted the third incident. 'Another time I entered a small village. A little boy was carrying a lit candle, making his way to the small temple nearby.' To tease the boy, Junayd asked him, 'Can you tell me where the light in your candle comes from? You lit this light yourself so surely you know the source of this light?' The boy laughed and said, 'Wait!' He blew out the candle in front of Junayd and said, 'You have seen the light go. Can you tell me where it has gone? If you can tell me where it has gone, I will tell you where it has come from, because it has gone to the same place. It has returned to the source.'

Junayd said, 'I had met great philosophers but nobody had made such a beautiful statement—It has gone to its very source. Eventually, everything returns to its source. A mere child made me aware of my own ignorance. I was trying to joke with the child, but the joke was on me. The light comes from nowhere, from nothingness, and it goes back to nowhere, to nothingness. Now, the final moment has come when the candle will go out, the light will go out and I know where I am going, to the same source. I remember that child with gratitude. I can still see him standing before me now, blowing out the candle. No situation is without a lesson. All situations are pregnant with meaning and intelligence. But we have to discover them. They may not always be on the surface. When we see life itself as our teacher and surrender to divine intelligence which is present in all things, these lessons become more accessible.'

The wisdom lies in the awareness that there is a reason for wherever we are. This is what surrender truly means. It is actually a surrender to presence; it is allowing things to be. You allow this moment, the way it is, as opposed to bringing in the idea of how it should be, how it could be, how it would be. There is a certain kind of relaxation, ease and freedom in operating from that state of being.

Ramakrishna Paramahamsa, a revered spiritual teacher, spoke of two ways in which one could go through life. One is like a baby monkey and the other like a kitten. The baby monkey will hold on with all its might to its mother as the mother jumps from one tree to the other. There is no question of letting go even for a moment, or it could fall and get injured or worse. So, this can be viewed as one way of going through life; hold on tight or you're going to fall down.

The kitten, on the other hand, just meows and the mother cat will come and pick it up from a special spot on the neck. When picked up in this way, the kitten will just suspend and relax its body. In the world of cats, the males are always looking to kill the kittens. So, the mother cats are always hiding the kittens from them and are constantly on the move. The path of the kitten is surrender. Your life is always in danger, but you have surrendered. Your mother is moving you from one spot to the next and taking care of you. On this path, you trust that whatever is happening is happening as it should, even though at times it might not seem so.

At one of my workshops, a lady told me that she had been laid off from work. The organization had downsized their workforce and some people had been made redundant. She said she was initially dejected and hurt since she had worked so sincerely, had given so many years of her life to the organization and here she was unceremoniously being kicked out of the company. She felt a terrible thing had happened to her, however, once she gathered herself, she wondered what she could do next. That exploration led her down a different path which was in far greater alignment with her deeper interests. She said she was so grateful for the journey she was forced to undertake that when she met her former boss, she shook his hand and thanked him for firing her. If it hadn't been for him, she would have never found her joy. Circumstances had forced her to ask herself what was really important, and now she was doing what she loved to do, and couldn't imagine a different life. Sometimes what may seem like a curse, upon reflection, may actually be a blessing. So, when something unwanted happens, it is a useful practice to say to yourself, 'I can't see it yet, but I'm sure there is some blessing hidden in this.'

I once saw a video of a wild elephant charging towards a man, but astonishingly, the man just calmly stood in his way. Unexpectedly, the elephant came to an abrupt stop midway and looked at him for a few moments and once again began to charge, but the man still stood where he was. Then the man beats his stick on the ground and the elephant now walked away. Perhaps the elephant could sense that this person was not afraid. Had the man run, he would have been crushed to death. He just stood there, and he was fine. If a charging elephant doesn't evoke a fight or flight response, then I don't know what will! The man knew from experience that if he stayed calm, the elephant would pick up on that energy. His thoughts were calm, and his body remained calm. Surrender is akin to floating on an infinite ocean of presence. As the man remained calm and present, he responded not from any sense of fear, but from complete clarity, trust and ease. This is the kind of power, protection and invincibility that is accessible in a state of surrender.

Byron Katie in her book *A Thousand Names for Joy*[17] narrates the story of her granddaughter Molly's birth. When her daughter Roxanne went into labour, everything was going well until suddenly the baby got stuck in the birth canal. She began to sink back into the womb and her heartbeat went into distress. The hospital was small and on that night at three in the morning, it was also understaffed. The doctor had no qualified assistant and there was a sense of panic in the room. He decided on an emergency Caesarean Section, brusquely dismissed the family and wheeled Roxanne into surgery. The mother-to-be was screaming in panic and the worried family feared that Roxanne and her baby were in life-threatening danger.

They asked Byron Katie if she would pray with them. In her book, she says she looked at their tired, frightened eyes and thought there was nothing she needed to ask for because she wanted whatever God wanted. She joined them, of course, and she took their hands, closed her eyes and stood there loving them, knowing how painful it can be to want a particular outcome. During this experience, she says there was no internal resistance and there was no fear. For her, reality was God. She says, 'I don't have to guess what God's will is. Whatever is happening is God's will. All I know is that God is everything and God is good.' In this case, it turned out that both Roxanne and the child were safe and well.

This is the essence of surrender. We trust that every atom in the universe is in the right place. We see that we don't always have the full picture and we trust what is emerging, including any resistance that we may have to it. We put down the burden of trying to control everything. We don't have to figure things out instantly. Sometimes the process of growth and awakening requires things breaking down in some ways. We all know that the seed has to break open for its potential to emerge. What seems like a catastrophe for the seed is the birthing of a tree.

Life keeps guiding us towards our full potential. There are three ways in which it does so—whispers, nudges and slaps. The most painless is when we get it intuitively, for example a still, quiet knowing within us that says—'Hey, you're not taking care of your health well enough. You need to exercise more, you need to get more rest, you need to eat better.' This is an example of a whisper.

When we ignore the whispers, then life guides us through nudges. This is when it shows up as emotions. If we are not tuned in, we miss them or we say, 'That's just a passing feeling.' However, if we neglect these nudges long enough, they become increasingly adamant. We experience irritation, sadness, heaviness, depression, anger and rage, often for what seems like no clear reason or in the form of a disproportionate reaction.

The third way in which life guides us when we ignore the previous two is in the form of a slap. This is when there are upheavals in our physical reality that we can no longer ignore. There is a bitter fight at home, somebody is diagnosed with a life-altering disease, we are made redundant at work. Now it's so big, we cannot sidestep it anymore. It's right in our face and we need to address it.

The universe is not vindictive, it is corrective. It gives us innumerable opportunities to rise to higher ground. If we neglect the whispers, then it will raise the tempo. If we ignore the nudges in the form of unpleasant emotions, it will give us bigger indications. Finally, when nothing else works, it will give us very strong indications, but it is compassionate. If we tune in to ourselves more and pay attention to our inner guidance, it will tell us what to do.

While we are trying to be more in tune with our inner guidance, how do we differentiate between intuition and impulse? We practise and we reflect. Every day is an excursion inside God's mind. We have to go through the process. You have to learn to discern: What does an impulse taste like? What does intuition taste like? What's coming from the heart? What is coming from the head? The whole process is to learn to live from presence and intuition. When you are completely in presence, you don't even need intuition because then you are literally one with everything. You are fully in alignment. No further guidance, adjustment or correction is needed when fully in alignment. Only when we are no longer in alignment do the whispers and nudges begin again, always to bring us back to presence.

'How will your mirror ever be polished if you complain with every rub?,' asks Rumi. Let us trust the process, surrender and wholeheartedly say—'Bring it on!'

Practices:

1. A straightforward surrender practice is to simply say 'Help!' and trust help will arrive. This is a responsive universe. If you don't know what the nudges of the universe are trying to tell you, then surrender and say, 'I don't know why this is coming up in my life. I have done my best. I don't know why this is happening. Please guide me. Please show the way,' and you will be shown the way. You will definitely be shown the way. A way will appear where earlier there was no way.

2. The opposite of surrender is control. This practice aims to identify the controller. Notice whether you have control over your sense experience to begin with. You realize that seeing is happening by itself. Hearing is happening by itself. Smelling, tasting, touching—are all happening by themselves. All kinds of processes in the body—respiration, digestion, elimination—are all happening without your control. So, the idea that 'I am in control of something' is just the work of imagination. Ask yourself the question—What do I control? Who is the controller?

Meditate on these questions.

20

Be

Diluted, only in the palmful of your day,
a moment,
carry it, into open waters, a gushing stream,
the stillness of a lake,
cup your hand and bring them to your lips,
can you taste your sadness still?

A needlepoint, in a vast unfolding tapestry,
patience, my love,
your tear-soaked reflection,
new patterns will come, new stories,
let them unfurl as they will,
each moment is you,
if only in dreams, mirages,
let it remain truthful, whole

It isn't given,
that you will be understood,
or that you will understand
or that, the ache of your heart will be soothed,
in the way that it needs
that you will be seen, your silence heard,
but what of it

The river finds its path, does it not,
without instruction,
as breath finds its way to life,
and trees, do they wait to be told how to flower,
which fruits to bear,
how deep their roots must go in search of what they need,
they simply are, as you must be,
in sadness or in joy, just be.

Resting as Awareness

When nothing is done, nothing is left undone.

—*Lao Tzu*

One of my teachers gave us a powerful example of effortless living. When we asked him, 'What is effortless living?', he said, 'Notice how hearing happens by itself. You don't have to make any effort to hear. Seeing happens by itself. Even if you don't have good eyesight, still seeing happens by itself. No effort needs to be made. Smelling, tasting and touch happen by themselves. The mind is also included in the sense doors, so thinking and perceiving happen by themselves as well. If you go a little bit deeper, breathing is happening by itself, the heart is beating by itself, digestion is happening by itself. If you look at it carefully, you realize everything is happening by itself. In fact, if you look carefully, even resistance is arising by itself. So, ask yourself this: 'Where does the notion that everything requires effort arise from?'

One of the most beautiful teachings is—effort is necessary until it isn't. This means that the only effort needed is to recognize that everything is happening by itself effortlessly. This takes a little bit of effort because that's not what we are accustomed to believing. We think we're making things happen and that we are the doer. It takes a certain amount of effort to steady our mind enough to notice how things are happening by themselves even though it may appear like we are making them happen. Many years ago, my teacher recommended I meditate intensely on the occasion of the solar eclipse. I was still in school at the time, and I was visiting my grandfather who lived in Jaipur. There was a room on the roof where nobody really came so I went to that room, and it was quite hot because it got direct sunlight. I sat there for eight hours straight apart from short bio breaks. That day I noticed more clearly than ever before how thoughts arise by themselves. 'Ah, I assumed I was the thinker, but these thoughts are thinking themselves.' It took some effort for me to experience effortlessness.

In one of the traditions, they call this data. Seeing is data, hearing is data; smelling, tasting and touching is data. There are literally trillions of data points. So many things we can see, smell, taste, touch and think. It's beyond a trillion. It's infinite. There's one thing in common with all these data points. There's one thread that connects every single one of them and that thread is that they arise within awareness. Something is aware of these things. Something is aware of pleasant and unpleasant. Something is aware of liked and disliked, wanted and not wanted, subtle and gross, near and far, known and unknown, understood and not understood, yours and mine—all these ideas, all these variances in this data. Another word we can use for that which knows data is—clarity.

If you're like most people, ninety-nine per cent of the day, your attention goes to data. We tend to focus on sensory experience and the mental formations around them—'I want to see more of this and less of this, hear more of this and less of this, smell more of this and less of this, taste more of this and less of this, touch and feel more of this and less of this.' Isn't this the game that goes on? Our pleasant sensory experiences instantly create pleasure and then cling to the pleasure. We want it to sustain and there is the fear—'What if I lose this?' The unpleasant experiences immediately create a kind of aversion—'I don't like this; I don't want this.' We want to push it away and there is a kind of dread, 'What if this stays forever?' The neutral experiences create a kind of restlessness because we are trying to get to the next peak. There is either anxiety or at the very least, boredom. Hence, the essence of spiritual practice is to detach from our hypnotic captivation with the data and come to clarity.

Clarity represents the effortless awareness which knows sensory data. When there is clarity, each moment has a different depth and dimension. Now data reveals awareness. Earlier the light of awareness was lost in data. Now every experience points back to awareness. Without awareness you could not feel what you are feeling. Every data point reveals and clarifies awareness. A common misunderstanding is that thinking or sensory experiences are a hindrance to meditation. However, meditation means resting as awareness and every data point pleasant or unpleasant, comfortable or uncomfortable, reveals awareness.

If you get this, you will be instantly free. Else you keep imagining a day will come when you only see pleasant things, hear pleasant things, feel pleasant things, smell pleasant things, think pleasant thoughts and that day my friend, is not going to come. And even if it does come, as we know, with pleasure, due to the law of diminishing marginal returns, the most delicious food tasted for the second time is not as nice and if we are fed the same thing every day, we are going to start hating it. So, we usually need to keep on upping the game with pleasure. When the pleasure is the same, we get used to and start taking it for granted. We need the next bigger hit. And at the peak, we can only go down, and we do know this at some level, which is why people get so disenchanted and wonder what the point of life is.

I would agree with this kind of thinking, but I don't agree with the despondency. This is because we have missed a crucial part of the equation which is 'sky-like' awareness within which all these clouds of experiences arise and pass away. So, instead of trying to find rest in what is transient, what if we turn our attention to the source of all experience?

Life is effortless. Everything is happening by itself. When effort is needed, effort will arise and when it is not needed it will not arise. This is not a complicated path. It is really very simple. I am offering you a map to enter a room you're already in. This is not about attaining anything. This is about recognizing and remembering. It's about uncovering what is already here. What is it like to rest as awareness, irrespective of data? By force of habit, we will be repeatedly hypnotized by data. We will get lost in thought and memory. That's all right because, as you know, just because the cloud covers the sun doesn't mean the sun has disappeared. So, there is no need for judgement. One of the great Tibetan masters was asked how this process works and he said it so beautifully, 'Glimpse after glimpse.' That's exactly how it works. Glimpse after glimpse, you penetrate the veil. Glimpse after glimpse, in this very moment, which is a timeless moment. This is not a function of time as time is also data.

Your perception of yourself, your personality, your so-called good habits, your so-called bad habits are all data arising within the infinite boundless expanse of clarity or awareness. These imaginary chains that you think you have; they're not going to get resolved. They're going to get dissolved. It's like waking up from a dream. You don't have to figure out how to solve the complicated problem of the dream. You simply awaken from the dream. How do you awaken from the dream? Awareness recognizes itself. It sees its own reflection in data. So, what's it like to relax the firm fist of effort and enter the dimension of effortlessness? What's it like to relax around any kind of pain and any kind of suffering? Take the word away from the experience, take away the word pain and take away the word suffering. It's just data revealing clarity.

In Tibetan Buddhism, this is called 'The View'. Once you have the view, the next step is to stabilize that view. This is called meditation. Short moments of resting in clarity repeated many times becomes continuous. The third step is action. Now, the meditation is not limited to the meditation seat or the duration of meditation. It completely penetrates your life, permeating and saturating every hidden corner of your being. It is meditation gone rogue.

This is where we start realizing that we aren't doing any of this. At some point, our ego has a scary realization. 'Oh my god! I'm not in control over here. I never was in control. I imagined I was and then I had the truth serum.' That is so scary for the ego. 'Oh, my goodness, I'm going to die.' Whereas it can't die because it was never there to begin with. It's just a misunderstanding. Until we awaken from the dream of separation. As we awaken, our whole universe awakens. It has no choice. Anyone or anything that encounters this awareness is seen as nothing but awareness. There is no clarity and data. There is only clarity.

Even if it seems you're deviating from what everyone has told you—your parents, your spiritual teachers—it turns out, that is also a part of your path. It's best said in the movie *Kung Fu Panda*, 'One often meets his destiny on the road he takes to avoid it.' This is where you start losing fear. You start even losing fear of fear itself. You're not even afraid to feel afraid. It's fascinating. It's okay to be afraid. It's okay to be anxious. It's okay to have a panic attack. Because you have discovered a deeper foundation, 'Nithya Shanti,' which means unshakable, unchanging, unassailable peace.

As you rest in that clarity, glimpse after glimpse, you realize there is no this and that. It's all for great benefit. You will have to unburden yourself of every single notion that you have. Every notion about what goodness is, what virtue is, what spirituality is, what attainment is, what enlightenment is. You must unburden yourself of all the scriptures you've read, all the theories, all the learning. What got you here, won't take you there. Yet, it was all needed, until it wasn't.

Everything will be seen as simultaneously a great teacher and a great poison. This is how you will transcend both the attachment to the teacher and the judgement of the poison, into a kind of undiluted freedom, the likes of which you could never have suspected. You could never have imagined it could even exist. This is a precious gift. Undistracted wisdom wrapped in undiluted love.

When the Buddha saw a ripe being, whether it was a monk or a householder, he would just say, 'Come and claim your inheritance. For too long, you have wandered.' This is your inheritance. You are not data. You are that which illuminates all data. All possible data. And that data is not separate from you. In essence, you are indescribable, shapeless, colourless, formless, timeless and without attributes. And yet, in expression, you are multiplicity. It's a play within a play. But when are you going to get the joke?

You can't get this if you believe that one thing is better than the other thing. Then you will play at kindergarten-level spirituality for a long time. May I have more of this. May I not have more of that. Prayer upon prayer. Please give me this. Please don't give me that.

You may still have a sense that you have chosen to read this book. You have chosen to make time for this. You have chosen to try to understand this. But let me assure you, this is also not your choice. The fact that you get to read something like this is the activity of grace. Not everybody gets to tune into this. Consider yourself the favourite child of the universe. Embrace it or don't embrace it, the treasures of the three worlds are now placed at your feet.

So, it's not your choice or even my choice. It is the activity of grace. Once in a very rare while, Shiva decides to remind himself. Buddha decides to remind himself. Krishna decides to remind himself. Christ decides to remind himself. Wake up. Wake up daughter. Wake up son. Claim your inheritance. Don't be a beggar in this world.

Data reveals clarity. Clarity reveals non-separation from data. Glimpse after glimpse. Short moments of resting as clarity many times become continuous. Even if you did not understand this, it's a very powerful re-patterning of your neural network even to just read this. Incorruptible seeds have been sown in the stream of consciousness, and they will sprout in their own beautiful, timeless time.

A Practice:

Right now, if you are reading these words and understanding them, something in you is doing that. You may say your eyes are seeing and the brain is processing it. But those are just organs. Something in you is receiving these words and understanding them. What is taking delivery of all different experiences? It could be pleasant or unpleasant. It could be wanted or unwanted. Our attention is always on the experience. Right now, focus on that which is receiving these experiences. You may call it awareness. You may call it consciousness. There is something that is aware. Focus on that even if it is unfamiliar. Something feels restless or rested. All the many life experiences; Where are they converging? Rest there.

Section 4

Daily Practices

Here are some practical ideas to help integrate the learnings from this book. It can be helpful to keep a journal where you record the practices you are doing and the benefits you have received and any questions that arise as you do them.

It is important to not be discouraged or give up, if for any reason your practice falters or gets interrupted. Remember that even if you just make a one per cent change every day, in just 100 days you will be completely transformed! Learn from all your challenges and interruptions, then smile and start again. Remember that this is a lifelong journey and every moment is a new opportunity to start afresh. No effort on the path of living consciously ever goes to waste. So, celebrate the smallest achievements and 'Catch Yourself Doing it Right!'

MORNING

Two min to five min: Practise any of the following before getting out of bed . . .

- Gratitude: Wake up with a smile, sit up in bed and start your day with the Lotus of Gratitude. Think of ten specific things you are grateful for. (one min)
- Power of intention: Vocalize, visualize, emotionalize the best possible outcome (BPO) to actualize a great day ahead. What we think about and thank about is brought about. (one min)
- Say three times: 'May I be a channel of blessings for someone today!' Feel the power of these words in your being. (one min)

- Practise the four-minute meditation: Breath, Feelings, Silence, Love.

Once you are out of bed . . .

- Practice *Mai Yur Ma* three times—wishing happiness for self, others and all beings.
- Greet yourself in the mirror and say something empowering such as: 'No matter what you have done, no matter what you have left undone, you are worthy of love!' or 'I choose to make this the happiest day of my life!'.
- Body care with mindfulness.
- Fifteen to thirty min: Perspiration: Simple exercises or walking outdoors.
  Fifteen to thirty min: Meditation: Enjoy just being.
  Fifteen to thirty min: Inspiration: Read or listen to something uplifting.

A helpful tip: Only turn on your mobile phone AFTER you have completed your morning routine!

DURING THE DAY

Practice any of the following:

- Make it a Complaint Free Day and 'Cancel!' all virus thoughts.
- Make it a Gratitude Filled Day. Say, 'How Wonderful!' no matter what happens.

- Power of Pause: Be aware of your breath and feelings.
- Eat Mindfully: Gratitude before meals. Savour food and chew thoroughly.
- Deep Listening: Pause, Question and Reflect.
- Remember the three Gates of Speech: Is it True? Is it Kind? Is it Necessary?
- Remember Rule #6! Don't take life so-oo seriously!

EVENING

- Clean up any residue of the day with Meditation, EFT, Ho'oponopono.
- Walk to complete 10,000 steps or make time for any exercise of your choosing.
- Family Time: Share experiences, listen, appreciate and hug your loved ones. Talk about the positive things that happened in the day. Play board games, read a book together, tell stories, sing songs, watch an inspiring film together.
- Instead of aimlessly getting on social media or watching TV, write a gratitude letter, call a friend, read a book, watch an inspiring documentary, or see short talks on subjects that interest you.
- Review the day and write in your journal.
- Plan the day ahead. This is a secret of highly effective people. Write down and visualize the day ahead before you go to sleep.
- Sit in bed with an attitude of gratitude. Say three times: 'I am so grateful for the blessings of this day. I choose to live and leave in the wisest possible way!'

Section 5

A Letter from Nithya

This is for you . . .

Now that you have been through these teachings and practices, I have a message just for you.

Something called you to this book and perhaps something called this book to you as well. Life seems to have this mysterious way of bringing to our attention what we need at every stage in our journey.

In my own process, I have felt guided and supported at every step. The more I have acknowledged, appreciated and relied on this guidance and support, the more unfailingly it has been there. I have had a sense that life knows my broadest intentions, even better than I myself do. I have learned to follow my curiosity and enthusiasm, and also trust that sometimes not getting what I want opens the doorway to something far more expansive and uplifting.

When I first began sharing these things, I was amazed at how different people were attracted to different teachings. Sometimes what was the most powerful idea for one person made little or no impression on another person. Different strokes for different folks, they say. This helped me realize that just because I resonate with something and find it helpful, it does not mean that others will feel the same way. However, everyone gets what they need in accordance with their deeper intentions and proclivities.

Similarly, in this book, many ideas and practices have been shared. Some might have been familiar before and some might be quite new to you. I suggest you trust your enthusiasm and practise the things that most call out to you. However, don't entirely dismiss what did not make sense or resonate on first pass. Some of the most transformational things I have come across actually did not appeal to me the first time I learned them. It sometimes took a while, even years before I could fully appreciate their depth and value.

The main thing I would like you to keep in your heart are these three words: 'Trust your process!' We would all like this path to be straight like an arrow. However, in most cases it tends to be a winding path, more like a spiral than an elevator. Again and again, we return to the same place and see the same things with new eyes. This is not a mistake. The journey is endless, yet the destination is now. We will discover for ourselves how everything is perfect and everything can also be improved.

Have a lot of patience. Infinite patience is the fastest way! Have a good sense of humour. It takes a great deal of maturity and wisdom to be able to laugh at oneself and not take oneself and life so seriously. We will fall a hundred times and rise a hundred and one times. The main thing I appreciate and admire in myself is my tenacity—the fact that I have kept my promise to myself, a promise that I will stick with the truth, I will stick with this path of awareness and love, no matter how long it takes to come to fruition. This is something I have done and continue to do. And this has made all the difference.

Our main obstacle is likely to be our self-doubts, or our overconfidence. Thinking various things about ourselves and others and life and then assuming that our thinking is automatically true! The reason this book is called 'Unburden,' is to remind us not to be fixated and make our thoughts and opinions our baggage. Just because a thought came visiting doesn't mean we have to serve it tea and entertain it! To abide primarily as awareness and love, instead of being identified with thoughts and feelings is the essential message of this book. We approach this in many different ways and offer various practices, yet it all comes down to this: shift from the story of your life and step into life itself—be one with life!

Every step on this pathless path of awareness and love we will be supported. The support will be directly proportional to our sincerity and earnestness. The deeper the asking, the faster and clearer will be the response. How come? Because the one answering the call is not far away in some other dimension. We are the ones we have been waiting for. Our innermost being is the one that unfailingly hears every intention, every prayer, every request, every longing, and so the response is immediate and unfailing. Our work is to be sincere and wholehearted. Let us begin by resolving to be honest, at least to ourselves. Be honest to yourself. Take off your masks and face yourself exactly as you are every day. Be naked. No excuses. No explanations. No judgments. No nothing. Meet yourself exactly as you are. This kind of inner honesty is the only thing that is needed. The rest will come. Without this, we cannot even take the first step.

So, I invite you on this adventure of consciousness. There are many more wondrous things to discover and uncover. You will find them all as you go along, and they will find you. The Buddha once held up a handful of leaves and asked, 'Monks, what is more: the leaves in my hand or the leaves in this great forest?' The monks were perplexed by this question and responded, 'Blessed One, the leaves in your hand are few, those in this great forest are countless!' The Buddha then responded, 'Just so monks, what I know through direct knowledge is like the leaves in the forest. What I share with you is like the leaves in my hand. Why so? Because this is enough for you to gain through direct experience all that you wish to know.' The monks delighted in his words.

This book is like a handful of leaves offered with love. Take the best, leave the rest. What has brought you so far will also lead you home. Unburden yourself of yourself. Again and again. Trust your process. Again and again. Be filled with the nectar of love and silence. May you be happy for a good reason and happy for no reason. May the rest of your life be the best of your life. And so it is. And so it is. And so it is!

The Highest in me, bows to the Highest in you!

Mai Yur Ma
Nithya Shanti

Section 6

Acknowledgements

Thank you to a stellar team who worked alongside us in bringing this book to life.

Padmajaa Iyer for her stewardship and for serving as a catalyst on this project.

Editors:

Smitha Sirivara
Lalitha Suhasini
Venkatraman Subramaniam (Gokul)

Transcribers & Reviewers:

Thank you Venkatraman Subramaniam (Gokul), Preethi Balan & Kavita Rajesh for managing the transcription & review process.

Aditi Anand
Aditya Dinesh
Ankur Shawney
Bhawana Mayor
Dr. Radhika Rawat
Lalitha Suhasini
Lavleen Riar
Madhumati Raju
Mani Bareja
Manisha Kalra
Monica Handa

Nikky Gandhi
Pallavi Shetty
Radha TSJ
Rashmi Nair
Reema Khanna
Ritika Dhir
Rivi Rebello
Smita Meher
Smitha Sirivara
Sudha Reddy
Vidya Rao
Vrinda Rathi
Zara Kaushik

Penguin Random House and Premanka Goswami for your belief in this book and for your friendship.

To our families, friends and well-wishers, our deep gratitude for all for your love and blessings.

References

[1] You can view a video that explains the EFT technique at this link: https://youtube/srmwOanJrBw

[2] Wilber, Ken. 1996. *A Brief History of Everything.* Boston and London: Shambhala.

[3] Dr. Schucman, Helen. 2007. *A Course in Miracles: Combined Volume.* Mill Valley: Foundation for Inner Peace.

[4] Sieden, Lloyd Steven. 1989. *Buckminster Fuller's Universe: His Life and Work.* New York: Basic Books.

[5] Bray Attwood, Janet and Ken Honda. 2015. *Maro Up: The Secret to Success Begins with Arigato: Wisdom from the "Warren Buffet of Japan".* Kindle Edition B018HDTZL6)

[6] Byron, Katie. 2002. *Loving What Is: Four Questions That Can Change Your Life.* New York: Harmony Books.

[7] Watch https://www.youtube.com/watch?v=bXuF8qmv5Nc (last accessed on 10 October 2021)

[8] Liberman, Jacob and Erik Liberman. 2001. *Wisdom from An Empty Mind.* Australia: Empty Mind Pubns.

[9] Buechner, Frederick. 1993. *Wishful Thinking: A Seeker's ABC.* New York: HarperOne.

[10] Prather, Hugh. 1983. *Notes to Myself: My Struggle to Become a Person.* New York: Bantam.

[11] Ashe, Arthur. 'His Success, Battle with HIV and Inspiring Reply to "Why Me?" Question', DNB Stories Africa https://dnbstories.com/2018/01/arthur-ashe-success-hiv-aids-true-story.html (last accessed on 10 October 2021)

[12] (http://nickreedent.com) *The Lady in Number 6*, An Oscar-winning documentary by Malcolm Clarke and Nicholas Reed, 2013.

[13] Bohm, David. 2002. *Wholeness and the Implicate Order.* New York: Taylor and Francis Routledge.

[14] Frankl, Viktor E. 1946. *Man's Search for Meaning.* London: Penguin Books Ltd

[15] Katie, Byron and Stephen Mitchell. 2018. *A Mind at Home with Itself.* New York: HarperOne

[16] Maharaj, Nisargadatta, author, Maurice Frydman, trans. 2012. *I Am That.* Durham: The Acorn Press.

[17] Byron, Katie and Stephen Mitchell. 2007. *A Thousand Names for Joy.* New York: Random House.